Creation According to the Scriptures:

A PRESUPPOSITIONAL DEFENSE OF LITERAL, SIX-DAY CREATION

EDITED BY

P. ANDREW SANDLIN

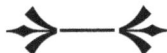

✦—✦

Copyright© 2001 by
Chalcedon

Printed on acid-free paper

Library of Congress Catalog Card Number:
ISBN 1-891375-12-1

Printed in the United States of America

Published by Chalcedon Foundation
PO Box 158
Vallecito, CA 95251

Table
of Contents

⇥ Introduction ⇤

HOW HIGH ARE THE STAKES?

By P. Andrew Sandlin

The debate over six-day creation within the "conservative" camp is surely not a tempest in a teapot. While it is fair to acknowledge that sincere Christians appear on both sides (pro and con) of the debate, it is not correct to deduce from this that literal, six-day creation is an issue on which there can be reasonable, brotherly disagreement. Latitudinarians who point out that there has been no consensus on this issue in the orthodox Christian church should realize that there is no consensus in the orthodox church on the doctrine of justification either, but that fact does not suggest we may hold a latitudinarian view on the doctrine of justification. We unswerving advocates of literal, six-day creation are not contending that those who disagree with us are not Christians. We are, however, contending that they are not believing in a Christian manner *on this issue*.

Theological controversy forces us to tighten up our understanding of the Bible. This is precisely how ecumenical orthodoxy came about. Harold O. J. Brown was correct to assert that, in this sense, heresy generated orthodoxy. It forced the church to solidify and formulate its understanding of the Bible on key controverted points. This is also true, as noted above, during the Reformation with the doctrine of justification by faith alone, as well as with the doctrine of Scripture alone as our revelational authority. The emergence of the Darwinian religion of evolutionism during the nineteenth century precipitated a crisis in the Christian church. Protestant liberals were easy prey for this religion and, in many cases, were at the forefront of its programmatic advance. But conservatives were not immune to its enticements, either. While, for example, Charles Hodge opposed it, his younger Princeton colleague, Benjamin Warfield, usually considered an exponent of Reformed orthodoxy, was dangerously soft on the issue. Warfield and other nineteenth-century Reformed luminaries have bequeathed to such conservative denominations as the Orthodox Presbyterian Church a toleration of views of the creation account that make concessions to the Darwinian religion. Many will deny this charge, countering that they are only seeking to be faithful to the Biblical text in denying literal, six-day creation. This is hard to believe. A straightforward understanding of the text can yield no other conclusion than that the world and all within it were made in six, twenty-four hour days. Yes, some preceded those on which the earth's sun was created, but this has no bearing on the length of the day itself. Elsewhere in the Bible we learn that God's command that man rest on the Sabbath day (a literal, twenty-four hour day) is anchored securely in the sequence of the six creation days and Sabbath day of the creation week. If the Jewish Sabbath was a literal, twenty-four hour day, the first Sabbath at the conclusion of the creation week was a literal, twenty-four hour day.

To those who argue that Moses was free to use figurative language in Genesis 1 and 2 in delineating the creation account, we counter that, first, we should accept the literal, straightforward language unless the text or the rest of the Bible gives us a reason to interpret it figuratively and, second, figures and tropes require a literal antecedent to give them meaning. In John 10, for instance, Jesus Christ tells us that He is the Good Shepherd of the sheep. These figures (shepherd and sheep) can have meaning precisely because of the previous existence of actual, literal shepherds and sheep. The figurative meaning rests upon the literal meaning. In Genesis 1 and 2, however, *there is no previous literal meaning upon which figurative meaning may be based.* Genesis 1 and 2 are, in fact, *laying out the literal meaning for much of the rest of the Bible.* The attack on literal, six-day creation is, thus, an implicit attack on the structure of Biblical revelation. Because in the Bible creation and redemption stand in an absolute historical continuum, attacks on the literal, historical character and language of Genesis 1 and 2 will, if consistently held, lead to attacks on the literal, historical character and language of Christ's great redemptive complex: birth, life, death, resurrection, ascension, session, and second coming. *Creation and redemption stand and fall together.*

In June of 2000, the Presbyterian Church in America, after several years of deliberation, concluded that it would not require that its ministers affirm literal, six-day creation. It thereby took the latitudinarian route and, thus, assured that, if not arrested, the denomination's movement will reach a destination denying the truth of Biblical infallibility and redemption. To those who scoff at such a "domino theory," that if one domino falls, they all will eventually fall, I gently point to the history of *every major Protestant denomination in the last three hundred years.*

Case closed.

⇥ Chapter 1 ⇤

THE IMPORTANCE
OF SIX-DAY CREATION

By R. J. Rushdoony

C reation is the initial doctrine we encounter in opening our Bibles, and it has been the point of initial attack of critics of Biblical Faith. The attack is almost as old as Christianity, because the early church moved in a Greco-Roman culture deeply committed to an evolutionary perspective. Aristotle as a scientist was deeply interested, as Cornelius Van Til showed us in a telling essay, in freaks because they represented a possible next step in evolution. More than a few of the early church Fathers, being pagan in origin, compromised on Genesis 1.

With the Enlightenment, the departures from an orthodox view of Genesis 1 became more common, and they were the starting point for the development of modernism. Today, in seminaries professing to be orthodox and created as protest against modernism, six-day creationism is held in contempt and compromising views are held.

All attempts to undermine strict six-day creationism have a deadly effect. First, they require a different view of the Bible. Orthodoxy has long held that the plain and obvious meaning of the text must prevail, not those meanings known only by scholars and apparent to none else. These novel kinds of exegesis deny the validity of the Reformation and the view of Scripture as given to the believer, not the scholar.

Second, a denial of six-day creation requires a different view of God. Process theology rapidly takes over and the Biblical God wanes as a humanistic and evolutionary "god" replaces Him. Biblical theology has waned with the rise of process theology. The expert replaces the common believer, and the Bible becomes a closed book.

Third, more than a few adherents of this shift can be called symbolic theology champions. They can read out of a text meanings which we, as men of simple faith, never can imagine are there! They are indeed a self-appointed elite in the world of the church.

Fourth, a grim division has been created by these attacks by the anti-six-day creationists between the seminary and the church. Thus far, the seminaries have prevailed, but a rebellion in some circles is brewing. It is important to note that the rapid growth of the church since the 1960s has been among churches bypassing the seminary. The seminary sees this as the triumph of ignorance, but many of these non-trained pastors have taught themselves Greek and Hebrew and more theology than the seminaries can boast of. A revolution is underway.

The issues in six-day creationism are thus more basic than many are willing to admit. The life of the church is at stake.

I pass at times in my travels a large stone church here in California. Seating about 1400, it was once full, but modernism killed it. The church which then purchased the structure started off well, until a seminary-trained fool gutted it with his modernism. It may soon need a third buyer!

⁂ Chapter 2 ⁂

THE OBJECTIVITY
OF BIBLICAL HISTORY

By P. Andrew Sandlin

DUALISM AND HISTORY

Τ he Bible does not present a fundamental dualism between heaven and earth, spirit and matter, and eternity and history. While God is the eternal, unchangeable, and transcendent being, He is exhaustively involved in His creation. Though fully distinct from His creation, He is in no sense sequestered from it. He is actively at work in the world moment by moment *(Col. 1:17; Heb. 1:3)*.

God created man in His own image *(Gen. 1:26-27)*, and man exists on the plane of history in the arena of God's cosmic actions. What theologians sometimes call "ordinary history" *(Historie)* is nothing other than the immediate sphere of God's dealings with man. The Bible knows nothing of a "suprahistory" or, in Bultmann's terms, "significant [existential] history" *(Geschichte)* of man's personal decision shorn of certain contact with "real" history (= history!). Even Cullman's "salvation history" *(Heilsgeschichte)*, referring to God's redemptive acts in history (history *as* revelation), is objectionable inasmuch as it creates a semantic distinction between the nature of these historical events and all others. In God's incomparable works of creation and redemption, not to mention His numerous miraculous acts recorded in the Bible, the sphere of His supernatural activity is the sphere of "normal" history. The earth on which man lives today is the same earth whose six-day creation Genesis 1 relates, though the present earth has been cursed because of man's sin. Christ's virgin birth, sinless life, vicarious death, bodily resurrection, and witnessed ascension all occurred in human history about two millennia ago. Though they were distinctly miraculous events, they were in no sense ethereal, suprahistorical events. The history in which we exist is the only history Christianity knows anything about.

St. John warned of those antichrists who claim that Christ had not come in the flesh *(1 Jn. 4:1-3)*. For nineteenth-century liberals, and many liberals today, the deity of Christ has been difficult to affirm. As faithless rebels, they cannot conceive how a man can be God. In large sectors of the patristic era, however, the problem was just the opposite: it was difficult to understand how God as Jesus Christ was actually a man.[1] Numerous Christological heresies (Docetism, for example) arose as an expression of this crucial misunderstanding. At many points the church was under pressure from Greek philosophy, which usually held that the body is the cage or capsule of the soul which is freed at death and that history is somehow dirty and inferior to the Forms or Ideals which are the Reality toward which man should strive. This introduced a fatal dualism from which the church was not exempt.[2] Human history necessarily suffers at the hands of this dualism, which always looks beyond history for true meaning and reality, while Christianity asserts that Christ as God of very God has entered history as Man of very man to reveal the fullness of God *(Col. 2:9)*.

Likewise, the Bible reveals our God as actively involved in history from the point of creation, and most intensely in the incarnational and redemptive work of Jesus Christ. To those Jews who doubted His messiahship, Jesus Christ asserted that He and the Father are one *(Jn. 10:30)*, to a doubting disciple He stated that to see Him was to see the Father *(Jn. 14:9)*, and the writer to Hebrews describes our Lord as the very image of the invisible God *(Heb. 1:3)*. Jesus Himself stated that no man may come to the Father except by Him (*Jn. 14:6*). Man cannot be saved apart from history, not merely because man himself is the object of God's creation, but primarily because Jesus Christ as a historical figure is the subject of man's redemption. Further, while human history will one day pass into eternity after the final judgment, man's existence will not be an ethereal spiritist mode. Rather, the Bible teaches the resurrection of both the just and the unjust, the just to everlasting life, the unjust to everlasting damnation (*Jn. 5:28-29; cf. 1 Cor. 15*). Contrary to popular evangelical belief, the Bible does not teach that the saints will live in a heaven "somewhere up in outer space." Rather, it teaches that God will purify and renovate the present earth, and that God will descend to dwell with men (*Rev. 21:1-3*). This will be heaven on earth, in its most absolute sense.

HISTORY, THE MEDIUM OF GOD'S REVELATION

History is the ordinary medium of divine revelation. To be sure, God in times past revealed Himself in dreams and visions as well as in direct contact with Moses on Sinai and St. Paul in the Arabian desert. But the first chapter of Hebrews informs us that in these "last days," the interadvental era, God has spoken to us in His Son, Jesus Christ — a discrete, historical figure. God's impeccable, infallible revelation is mediated to man in the historically anchored Holy Scripture, as well as the historically anchored Son of God, Jesus Christ. It is true that some of the "history as revelation" school stress the revelational character of history to the exclusion of Scripture as the infallibly definitive interpretation of history. And so-called evidentalists hold that even the miraculous events of redemptive history are self-interpreting, not requiring the attestation and interpretation of Holy Scripture. These deviant viewpoints, however, must never corner us into adopting the opposite error of perceiving the Christian Faith, human salvation, and Holy Scripture as merely rational, experiential, intuitive, or "supra-historical" matters not securely anchored in God's pre-destinating concrete historical dealings.[3] For Christianity, history is an objective fact.[4]

ASSAULTS ON THE OBJECTIVITY OF BIBLICAL HISTORY

Most modern assaults on the objectivity of Biblical history among those who nonetheless claim a measure of fidelity to the Bible's authority spring from an alleged alertness to literary analysis. Clark Pinnock, for example, who once embraced and articulated the highest form of Biblical authority,[5] states in a more recent work:

> Starting with some Old Testament examples, indications of the special character of the Bible's historical writing crop up again and again. At the very beginning, we are confronted with a six-day creation and begin to wonder how the world can have been created in so short a time. When we look for other explanations, we soon notice the internal parallelism of the days (days one to three describe spheres, and four to six point to inhabitants of those spheres) and contextual factors (the need to correct the theology of the Babylonian myths of creation). The problem seems to have been a misunderstanding of the literary genre. In the narrative of the fall of Adam, there are numerous symbolic features (God molding man from dirt, the talking snake, God molding woman from Adam's rib, symbolic trees, four major rivers from one garden, etc.), so that it is natural to ask whether this is not a meaningful narration that does not stick only to factual matters.[6]

Rather, it is natural to ask whether Pinnock's is not a patent attempt to subvert Biblical history by employing a fundamentally unbelieving hermeneutical method. This questioning or dismissal of revelation which the orthodox have routinely understood as referring to actual, discrete history is especially notable because Pinnock is regarded as an evangelical. Theological liberals have long questioned the objectivity of Biblical history on the grounds that such history — and especially the miracles of Biblical history — conflict with notions of the modern scientific and historical world view; in short, these narratives of Biblical history simply seem incredible to the modern mind.[7] Evangelicals like Pinnock are not far behind in this race to undermine Biblical history. Their unbelief, one should note, is compatible with the loudest professions of adherence to formal Biblical authority,[8] a fact from which we can deduce that "formal Biblical authority" is insufficient to guarantee maintenance of Biblical religion. If, for example, one claims that the Bible is certainly the infallible Word of God and *also* that a proper hermeneutical treatment requires the symbolic interpretation of Genesis 1-11, a "metaphorical" virgin birth of Christ, or a "spiritual" resurrection of Christ, the claims of Biblical infallibility are meaningless and in fact hypocritical. A *material* Biblical authority sets forth *the type of book the Bible is* and the type of message it teaches, not merely *that* it is infallible. The orthodox hold that the outline of this message is enshrined in the Christian creeds, and that the divine message itself is expressed in, for the most part, simple, straightforward language in the Bible. It certainly includes figures of speech, but the language itself is ordinary language. Contrary to Pinnock, there is no "special character of the Bible's historical writing." If there were, Biblical interpretation and understanding would be the province of literary specialists, not the vast majority of Christians who lack (and have historically lacked) special literary training. In other words, *the attempt to hold Scriptural meaning hostage to "special . . . historical writing" is a form of gnosticism.* Biblical authority, to put it another way, is not merely a statement about the Bible's infallibility without reference to its meaning (mathematics textbooks, strictly speaking, may be infallible); rather, to assert the infallibility of the Bible is to claim that it speaks the unvarnished truth in ordinary human language; this is not a hermeneutical or exegetical induction, but a presupposition for approaching the Bible in the first place. Those who would counter that to insist on ordinary history and ordinary language is to impose our own views on the Bible are really contending that God has not been pleased to disclose Himself to man as made in God's image, but only to a certain *kind* of man — one initiated into the gnosis of sophisticated literary analysis; this denies catholicity, a cornerstone of the Faith, and is anti-Christian to the core. The Faith subsists in ordinary history and the Bible speaks in ordinary language. Attempts to posit a special revelational language or a special revelational history subvert the Faith; they revive the spirit of antichrist.

CAPITULATION TO THE PREVAILING THOUGHT FORMS

This assault on the orthodox understanding of the accounts of Biblical history is often accompanied by a diminution in the confidence of Biblical reliability or an attempt to appease the baying hounds of "scientific" sophistication of the modern era. A prime example is Meredith Kline, who states in the introduction to a recent article delineating his attack on the literal, six-day creation account of Genesis 1:

> To rebut the literalist interpretation of the Genesis creation week propounded by the young-earth theorists is a central concern of this article.... The conclusion is that as far as the time frame is concerned, with respect to both the duration and sequence of events, the scientist

is left free of biblical constraints [*sic!*] in hypothesizing about cosmic origins.[9]

The implicit assumption seems to be that if we can eliminate an antiquated, constraining orthodox view of Biblical creation, we may with a great sigh of relief give modern scientism (the religion of science) free reign. One ponders whether it is possible to invent entire, structured, interpretative applications for the express or implied purpose of paying homage to the modern ethos. Unfortunately, it is. Mark Noll, for instance, championing B. B. Warfield's toleration of the evolutionary religion, holds that natural revelation (interpreted, of course, by "the consensus of modern scientists, who devote their lives to looking at the data of the physical world"[10]) is the key to understanding the Biblical [!] teaching regarding issues of modern science. We can expect this angle from modern evangelicalism, for whom Scripture is not and never has been the epistemological authority in terms of which all of life (including science) must be interpreted.[11] In referring to the doctrine of creation as an example of "damaging intellectual habits of fundamentalism,"[12] Noll is really connoting that those who espouse the straightforward Biblical account of creation refuse to surrender, in Kline's terminology, "[B]iblical constraints in hypothesizing about cosmic origins." Noll holds that in their tenacity, these "fundamentalists" are simply reflecting the "common sense" scientific approach of the nineteenth century,[13] though this would not explain why Christians in *earlier* generations embraced creationism. Perhaps, moreover, it did not occur to Noll how his own "historically situated" assaults on creationism may not simply be — *must* be — instances of worship at the shrine of historical relativism and the lust for academic respectability among moderns for whom the scandal of Christ, the Bible and the orthodox Faith *(Gal. 5:11)* will never be respectable.

Theologians like Noll and Kline undermine the Faith and the church. Impressionable youth not sufficiently grounded in orthodoxy, dogmatics, exegesis, and ecclesiastical history are supple prey in the hands of such men who turn out entire generations of religious latitudinarians for whom Biblical history may be surrendered if it conflicts with the latest scientistic fads. We have a name for this: *apostasy.*

Of course, Biblical literary analysts who undermine the orthodox conception of Biblical history may accuse their orthodox opponents of confusing hermeneutics with history or theology: the intent is not to diminish Biblical history, they say, but to highlight Biblical language. It is not hard to detect the fatal flaw of this idea. For were all of the Bible interpreted, for example, mythically, or according to the canons of modern literary analysis, it would be possible to undo *every single* aspect of Biblical history. Then the Bible would be nothing but an interesting spiritualizing and moralizing storybook. Actually, what "post-conservative" evangelicals like Clark Pinnock and Stanley Grenz are proposing sounds quite similar at points to just this "narrative" notion.[14] The Bible then becomes little more than a Semitic literary document whose contact with the history in which it arose is not always clear.

It all boils down to the issue of what sort of book the Bible really is. Orthodox Christians hold that it is the inspired and infallible Word of the Living God issuing from eternity but arising within specific historical situations and bound inextricably to human history. This does not imply that the orthodox view of Scripture requires a uniform literalism at all points, defying tropes — like metaphor, simile, allegory, and so forth. The Bible is literally true, but not all of the Bible is true literally. But, as Noel Weeks insightfully observes, tropes are possible only because they refer to some prior concrete historical phenomenon. This fact holds special significance for those who repudiate the literal, six-day creation account of Genesis.[15] The *structure* of the Bible's message is not tropological; it is straight-forward literature — even in its tropes — and designed to be read by believers of all walks of life.[16]

Biblical history, moreover, is a seamless robe. To deny the historicity of the Genesis account of creation is to establish the groundwork for an equally plausible denial of Jesus Christ's historical redemptive minis-try. Biblically, creation and redemption stand in an absolute continuum. This fact is evidenced not only by Jesus Christ's direct reference to the creation account as an actual, discrete historical event and Adam and Eve as actual, discrete historical individuals *(Mt. 19:4-6)*, but also by the clear implications of the striking representational parallelism in Romans 5: Adam, the first man, plunges the entire human race into sin while Christ, the Second Adam, restores to the elect the sta-tus Adam lost. Christ acts for the elect, not only in His full deity, but also in His full humanity — because Adam as fully man acted for those whom He represented (the entire race) in choosing sin and depravity, so Christ as fully man acted for those whom he represented (the elect) in leading them into justification and righteous-ness. To deny the discrete humanity of Adam is not merely to subvert the verbal and situational parallel-ism of this passage; it is to undercut Christian salva-tion. In short, the historicity of Adam is one of the hinges on which Christian soteriology swings. This is only one example of how a supposed "literary approach" to Scrip-ture readily subverts Biblical religion.

CONCLUSION

Biblical history — including the creation account — is *history*. It is the objective history in which we presently subsist. There is no other history. Further, to assail accounts of Biblical history by appeal to mod-ern hermeneutical methodologies is to deny Biblical infallibility and subvert the Faith. If we are to preserve the Faith, we must draw the line *here*.

REFERENCES

1 Harold O. J. Brown, *Heresies* (San Francisco, 1984), 27.

2 Andrew Louth, *The Origins of the Christian Mystical Tradition From Plato to Denys* (Oxford, 1981).

3 Geerhardus Vos, "Christian Faith and the Truthfulness of Bible History," in ed., Richard B. Gaffin, Jr., *Redemptive History and Biblical Interpretation: The Shorter Writings of Geerhardus Vos* (Phillipsburg, NJ, 1980), 458-471.

4 This does not imply that history is self-interpreting, or that Biblical revelation is unnecessary, or that one may appeal to bare history for apologetic purposes. As Van Til notes, natural revelation and supernatural (propositional) revelation were designed from the beginning to be complementary, "Nature and Scripture," in eds., N. B. Stonehouse and Paul Woolley, *The Infallible Word* (Philadelphia, 1946), 255-275.

5 Clark H. Pinnock, *A Defense of Biblical Infallibility* (Nutley, NJ, 1967).

6 *idem.*, *The Scripture Principle* (San Francisco, 1984), 119.

7 L. Harold DeWolf, *The Case for Theology in Liberal Perspective* (Philadelphia, n. d.), 31-43.

8 Editorial [Kenneth Kantzer], "Rhetoric About Inerrancy: The Truth of the Matter," *Christianity Today*, September 4, 1981, 16-19.

9 Meredith G. Kline, "Space and Time in the Genesis Cosmogony," from *Perspectives on Science and Christian Faith*, 48:2-15, 1996 [American Scientific Affiliation]; Kline's earlier and less audacious piece is "Because It Had Not Rained," *Westminster Theological Journal* 20 (1958), 146-157.

10 Mark Noll, *The Scandal of the Evangelical Mind* (Grand Rapids, 1994), 207, cf. 196-208.

11 An idea opposed fully by Cornelius Van Til, *The Defense of the Faith* (Phillipsburg, NJ, 1967 edition), 8 and *passim*.

12 *ibid.*, 208.

13 *ibid.*, 199.

14 Millard Erickson, *The Evangelical Left* (Grand Rapids, 1997).

15 Noel Weeks, *The Sufficiency of Scripture* (Edinburgh, 1988), 105.

16 In contradistinction to the "interpretive maximalism" of *e. g.*, James Jordan, *Judges* (Tyler, TX, 1985), xi-xvii. Jordan contends that man's existence as God's created image requires a symbolic approach to the Bible's message. One may have thought that it denoted just the opposite: man thinks in a creaturely (analogically, not univocally) way, just as God thinks the Creator's way.

⊹ Chapter 3 ⬧

EVOLUTIONARY FAITH

By Mark R. Rushdoony

For by him were all things created, that are in heaven, and that are in earth, visible and invisible, whether they be thrones, or dominions, or principalities, or powers: all things were created by him and for him: And he is before all things, and by him all things consist. (Colossians 1:16-17)

harles Darwin did not originate the idea of a world without God. Sinful men longed for such a world since the first rebellion. All Darwin did was give a seemingly scientific explanation that made the idea sound biologically possible. The result was that men flocked to his theory. They wanted to believe in a world without God, or at least in a world where He was reduced to a useful addendum. The Enlightenment claim was that man is in his essence a rational creature. Man does have a mind and does reason, but is essentially a religious creature, Scripture tells us. He is a creature of faith. Man can think only in terms of what he believes. We understand a man when we understand what he believes. Darwin assumed God did not create, and many who longed for such an existence independent of divine origin flocked to this faith. Those who believe Scripture assume God did create and admit this as an article of faith.

WHAT SCIENCE CANNOT DO

Evolutionists begin with the assumption that evolution happened, then deny that this assumption is a faith. When opposed they must appear logical (reasonable), so they define science in an entirely self-serving way. They define God and the supernatural out of the realm of science and then smugly declare their faith to be the only "scientific" explanation. It is true that the scientific method is based on what is measurable, observable, and repeatable; but those criteria are never the sole determination of what is real or what happened in the past. Science constantly tries to work with a given historical reality without feeling the need to prove the historical act that precipitated it. The argument that science is limited cannot be used as grounds to deny what is beyond those limits. It only proves there are limits to what science can or cannot prove.

The whole concept of origins is, in fact, beyond the limits of what is measurable, observable, or repeatable. Either evolution or Divine creation must therefore be accepted by faith. Origins involve historical events not subject to the scientific method. Does that mean our world and life had no origin because it cannot be subject to the scientific method? Evolutionists say Divine, miraculous origin is non-scientific but that their own faith in origins by "natural" processes (no longer observable) is. Far too many have allowed themselves to be intimidated by such a self-serving summary rejection of their Faith for another faith.

EVOLUTION'S BORROWING OF CHRISTIAN CAPITAL

The evolutionary faith must borrow Biblical ideas and adopt them. The idea of the eternal is merely transferred from God to matter. Evolution cannot explain the origin of matter, so God must be reluctantly accepted as a first cause of matter (and then forever limited to the realm of religion), or it must be postulated that matter itself is eternal. Evolution simply cannot explain the origin of matter. It must be their starting point.

Intelligent design by the Creator is also transferred to the natural realm. The "Laws of Nature" take the place of Divine design. Evolutionists often absurdly ascribe foresight, intent, and intelligent development to biological processes or creatures themselves. Thus a creature is said to have "adapted itself," "developed the ability," or "evolved a unique organ which allows. . . ."

Since evolution posits life from non-life, it must also borrow the idea of the miraculous. What is not possible is said to be plausible if it occurred over a long time. Inheritance of acquired characteristics, natural selection (Darwin's idea), and mutation-selection have been suggested as entirely different methods for these changes to take place. The fact that the entire "scientific" basis of Darwin's theory has since been discredited as a means of changing species is itself a powerful witness to the fact that evolution is based on a faith that survives its science being discredited and revamped.

CHRISTIAN COMPROMISE

There has been a trend in this century for Christians to abandon Genesis 1-11 as scientifically or historically accurate. By various means and reasoning they make concession to the evolutionary faith. But they have not thereby gained the respect of evolutionists, and why should they? They have merely tacked God onto another faith. But the Biblical idea of a Sovereign who controls time and eternity is inconsistent with evolution. When creation is transferred to the inherent physical nature of matter, sovereignty and power are also transferred. God becomes an outsider to nature. If God is not the Creator, in what way can He claim any right or interest in the creation or in us as creatures?

Evolution and Christianity are different faiths that have mutually exclusive claims. Evolution posits matter that made man who made his gods. Any attempt to accommodate this view with Scripture places God in a subordinate role. It also destroys the integrity of Scripture because it claims two sources of truth. The Bible is seen as a source of spiritual truth and nature is seen as the source of scientific truth. But this is dualism. It posits two sources of truth from two gods. But inevitably one will be favored and given preeminence. Since this position began with accommodation to evolution, further surrender becomes a criteria of respectability. Once evolutionary faith is accepted, nature is our source of knowledge about science, and the Bible is increasingly ruled out. We are left with man's reason and nature. If only the divine is excluded, only the natural is left. Evolution is an exclusive faith that defends itself by excluding all others.

Darwin offered men who wanted freedom from God an "out." He provided an account of origins which provided miracles but was impersonal, materialistic, and held no man to account. Men felt freed from the Creator and creaturehood. Once God is a creation of evolved men, He may be accepted, rejected, or limited by those men at will. Truth is a premise of human thought. There are no "brute facts." Facts have significance because meaning is a part of God's Creation. Without God there can be no meaning or truth. Man accepts or rejects the God of Scripture as an expression of his religious nature, but he must posit an eternal order. If he rejects God as Creator, he will posit an origin and truth without God. Creation or evolution are the only alternatives as origins. Men structure their thoughts on one of these faiths.

We must challenge any artificial definition of science, which would remove God from His Creation. Evolution offers billions of years of chaos and chance but then borrows Christian ideas of law and truth. Men cannot escape faith; they only choose another. Evolutionary faith is the faith of rebels against God and represents that rebellion and irrationalism in the name of science.

⟶ Chapter 4 ⟵
THE WAR AGAINST GENESIS 1
By Mark Ludwig

EVOLUTIONARY MYTHOLOGY

Many of the world's religions include some story of creation in their mythology simply because where we come from has a direct bearing on how we must live. If man is the fertility god's creation, then he should serve the fertility god. If man is a cosmic accident then he need answer to no one, and he may serve himself. If man is Yahweh's creation, then he should serve Yahweh. If Yahweh is a lawgiver, one must serve Him with obedience. If He is merciful, His servant should be merciful, and so forth.

As such, the Biblical creation story has been a bone of contention at least since Christianity began to confront the gods of Greece and Rome in the first century.

In many respects, we have to understand the current evolutionary world view as just this kind of mythology. Operational science makes predictions about how the universe operates. Such predictions can be falsified by experiments. For example, Newton's law of gravitation makes exact predictions about how a body of mass M attracts another body of mass m. For example, it can be used to calculate the trajectory of a ball thrown up in the air. If Newton's law weren't true, one could perform an experiment to demonstrate that fact. In other words, one could throw the ball and clearly see that the predicted trajectory was not the same as the actual trajectory, within some reasonable margin of error. Thus, Newton's law is falsifiable.[1]

Current evolutionary "theory" is not capable of making any significant falsifiable predictions. For example, it is utterly incapable of predicting how various organisms will evolve with time, except for the absolutely simplest, most obvious changes. As such, one runs into all kinds of problems when trying to apply evolutionary "science" to artificial genetic self-reproducing systems. For example, modern "theories" don't give the scientist any clue of what to expect in the development of computer viruses.[2] A computer virus is a self-reproducing entity which passes genetic information (in the form of machine code) from one generation to the next. As such, it should be subject to Darwinian evolution. Will viruses evolve in an unending upward spiral and eventually take over the world's computer systems? Computer professionals do not currently take such threats seriously, although such a scenario is certain if we apply the same kind of reasoning to computer viruses that is applied every day to the real world of carbon-based organisms.

Is this intellectual schizophrenia? The truth is that we do not need evolution to explain the existence of computer viruses because everybody "knows" they have creators. People write computer viruses, so postulating a creator causes no philosophical or religious repercussions. At the same time, evolution is demanded of carbon-based organisms because creation is unpalatable for philosophical reasons.

In the end, we must understand evolution as a scientism, or mythology couched in scientific terms. It is a great tool for explaining away the past because, lacking solid predictive power, it can explain any historic scenario presented for analysis. Once one realizes that evolution is a mythology, one can begin to better understand its success in the past 140 years. Belief in it has become so widespread, not because of scientific evidence or predictive ability, but because its mythology caters to the wishes of sinful man.

THE HISTORY OF THE EVOLUTIONARY MYTHOLOGY AND THE DECONSTRUCTION OF GENESIS

Evolutionary ideas were born in a society that was formally Christian, but inwardly rebelling against the constraints of Scripture. The nineteenth century was the century of Victorian prudishness, of teetotalers, temperance revivals and a proliferation of quasi-Christian cults which sought a "higher" form of godliness in laws of purely human origin. It was also the century of lewd romanticism, universalism, and deconstructionist thought of every kind, ranging from theology to philosophy to government to science.

The Victorian mindset was revealed only too clearly with the anonymous publication of *Vestiges of the Natural History of Creation*[3] in 1844, a book which presented a complete evolutionary world view ranging from cosmology to the origin of man, without the slightest pretense of scientific accuracy. Rather, the author simply engaged in every manner of wild speculation. The book was publicly condemned by biologists, geologists, and theologians alike. However, *Vestiges* became a bestseller overnight, going through ten editions in ten years.

In response to scientific (and even not-so-scientific) challenges to the traditional Biblical view, the deconstruction of Genesis 1 began in earnest. Deconstruction took the form of denying the literal truth of the creation story and turning it into a myth. This program was not carried out by atheists or agnostic scientists, but by so-called Christian thinkers who retreated from literal interpretation in order to accommodate the supposedly indisputable facts.

For example, in 1833 Charles Lyell published his famous treatise on uniformitarian geology, *The Principles of Geology*. Up to that time, geological formations were largely interpreted in terms of catastrophes, the Noahic flood being the most important. Lyell attempted to bring geology into the realm of day-to-day natural cause and effect. His gradualist approach required an immense age for the earth, at least millions of years. As a result, geologists were divided into two camps, catastrophists and gradualists. The catastrophists largely adhered to the idea of a young earth, while the gradualists advocated an old earth.

Once *Vestiges* was published, however, Lyell appeared conservative in comparison. So when Hugh Miller, editor of *The Witness*,[4] published his *Footprints of the Creator* (1847) as a popular response to *Vestiges*, he appeared to be defending the Faith. However, to Miller, defending the Faith largely meant putting down the evolution of the species, and especially the evolution of man from monkeys. His great objection was rightly that man's soul could not scripturally be the same as an animal's, as evolution would seem to imply.

Miller had already embraced the idea of a progressive, Lyellian fossil record where the simplest organisms came first.[5] In both *Footprints* and *Testimony of the Rocks* (1856), Miller held to the idea of the progressive fossil record, but maintained that it did not thereby prove evolution since the fossil record does not show continuous gradations from one life form into another. Rather, complex life forms appear quite suddenly in finished form.

In effect, Miller was giving both the ordinary believer and the scientist theological room to accept the idea of an old earth and a generally progressive fossil record without discarding his faith. In so doing, he had to discard Genesis 1 as literal. In place of the Creator of Genesis 1, Miller's God was a God of the gaps, a Creator who, at various times in the long epochs of history, created fish, amphibians, reptiles, birds, mammals, and, finally, man.

Neither was Miller alone in giving way to science. German higher criticism was invading England at the same time and so-called scholars were actively questioning their faith in a much broader context than evolution. To put Darwin in context of his times, *Origin of the Species* was published in November, 1859. Another book, not so well-remembered today, *Essays and Reviews*, was published just months later, in February, 1860. *Essays and Reviews*, authored by liberal Anglican clergymen, is generally acknowledged as the "coming out" of higher criticism in England. In a climate of theological upheaval, it is hardly surprising that novel ideas like evolution would find supporters in the church. Indeed, it would appear that *churchmen were more eager to compromise with Darwin than scientists.*

The pattern of scientific "advance" followed by compromising Scripture to accommodate the supposed facts has been repeated again and again from the mid-nineteenth century right up to the present. Roman Catholic scholar Saint Georges Mivart advanced the idea of theistic evolution in a book *The Genesis of Species* and concluded that "Christian thinkers are perfectly free to accept the general evolution theory."[6] In the same year, the president of Princeton University affirmed evolution in *Christianity and Positivism.*[7] In 1898 R. A. Torrey hinted that evolution might be true of animals.[8] In 1907 A. H. Strong wrote that "neither evolution nor the higher criticism has any terrors to one who regards them as part of Christ's educating process."[9] In 1911 B. B. Warfield said that, while evolution is not a substitute for creation, it can "supply a theory of the method of divine providence."[10] In *The Fundamentals* James Orr defends theistic evolution and calls it "creation from within."[11] E. C. Messenger's *Evolution and Theology* (1954), very influential in Roman Catholic circles, argued that Scripture did not conflict with even purely natural evolution. Likewise, Bernard Ramm's *The Christian View of Science and Scripture* (1954), very influential in evangelical circles, advocates old-earth progressive creationism or theistic evolutionism. In the more "progressive" extreme, there is the infamous Pierre Teilhard de Chardin (1881-1955), a

Roman priest who became one of evolution's most visible, vocal, and effective promoters within Christian circles, both Protestant and Roman Catholic. Teilhard de Chardin is notable for his radical evolutionism and absolute statements like "Evolution is a light illuminating all facts, a curve that all lines must follow"[12] and "it is Christ who is saved by Evolution."[13] This list is a mere sampling of what has passed for theology since Darwin's time.

MEREDITH G. KLINE'S CONTRIBUTION TO THE MODERN MYTHOLOGY

So theologians, preachers, and Christian scholars have been the forerunners in radically deconstructing Genesis 1 in modern times. That deconstruction continues in liberal circles to this day, as Christians seek to nail the exegetical lid on the coffin of Genesis 1. An important example is Meredith G. Kline, of Westminster Theological Seminary, Escondido, California. Kline is intent on putting down both the literal Genesis creation week as well as the day-age view, leaving the scientist "free of biblical constraints in hypothesizing about cosmic origins."[14] Kline's deconstructionism is important to consider because it has been accepted and promoted in a number of popular books on creation/evolution for Christians.[15]

Kline's argument is that Genesis 2:5 invalidates an understanding of Genesis 1 in terms of sequential events, be they literal days or long periods of time, and demands that it be understood in literary terms, not at all suggesting a sequence of events.

To understand Kline's argument, let us first examine Genesis 2:4, 5. The American Standard Version[16] reads:

These are the generations of the heavens and of the earth when they were created, in the day that Jehovah God made earth and heaven. And no plant of the field was yet in the earth, and no herb of the field had yet sprung up; for Jehovah God had not caused it to rain upon the earth: and there was not a man to till the ground.

Working with the ASV, Kline asserts that this verse ascribes the reason for a lack of plants to (a) the lack of natural rain water or (b) the lack of a man to provide some form of artificial irrigation. Kline traditionally divides God's works into those of creation and providence, and then asks the question whether the works of providence were different during the creation week than they were after it. Genesis 2:5, he says, is proof that they were not: "The Creator did not originate plant life on earth before he had prepared an environment in which he might preserve it without bypassing secondary means and without having recourse to extraordinary means such as marvelous methods of fertilization."[17]

Now, Kline argues, if the creation week were a literal seven-day week of 24-hour days, such a statement in Genesis 2:5 would make no sense, because it would hardly matter if plants didn't get rain for a fraction of a day on an earth covered with water just a day before.

Alternatively, the day-age theory, in which each day of creation is understood as a long, unspecified period of time, would not make sense because it would require plants to exist without sun or moon for an indeterminately long period of time. That would require some extraordinary biological phenomenon, whereas Genesis 2:5 takes for granted only ordinary phenomena.

This argument is sufficient for Kline, a theologian, to conclude that Genesis 1 cannot, therefore, be understood in literal or even sequential terms. Using the exegetical principle of Scripture interpreting Scripture, he concludes that "the literalness of the sequence is no more sacrosanct than the literalness of the duration of the days in this figurative week."

To further explain the figurative days of Genesis 1 without writing the whole chapter off as mythology,

Kline invokes a Gnostic duality in what he calls a "two-register cosmology" (e.g., the supernatural world, or heaven, and the natural world, or the universe). The days of Genesis 1, he argues, refer to heaven's time, and not to any sequence of events on earth. Yet the heart of Kline's argument is still in his exegesis of Genesis 2:5.

Does Kline's reasoning stand up to scrutiny though? If Genesis 2:5 does indeed imply that only the usual means of providence were in operation during the time of creation, then any understanding of creation as a process protracted much beyond a week gets into quick trouble.

In any long-period creation, there would have been a long period after the formation of the earth and the appearance of dry ground during which there were no plants. Bringing Genesis 2:5 into the picture suggests that there were no plants because there was no rain. However, one has to wonder what extraordinary processes could have been at work during this long period to prevent rain on the earth? Likewise, what extraordinary process, in the absence of rain, could have broken down bare rock into the earth required for plant life?

If normal physical processes were operating during the creation period, rains would have begun within a day or so, unless (a) there was no water in the oceans (contrary to Scripture and all scientific evidence) or (b) there was no sun or other strong light source to evaporate the water. Kline properly rejects the idea of a sunless world for a long period of time, simply because if normal physical processes were operating, plants would die without it. Presumably, he would likewise reject a waterless world.

This presents a paradox which Kline seems to have ignored. According to Kline, Genesis 2:5 demands normal physical processes, but no rain. Yet normal physical processes would cause rain in about a day.

The only way to resolve this paradox is (a) to abandon the assertion that Genesis 2:5 demands normal physical processes during the creation period, or (b) to return to a short period of time — about a week — for creation.[18]

Neither is this the only paradox Kline faces. Genesis 2:5 ascribes the lack of vegetation to both a lack of rain *and* the lack of a man to till the ground. In his argument, Kline quietly replaces the "and" with an "or" in order to support his naturalistic thinking. Yet the "and" would suggest that man was part of God's providence for the earth, so God did not plant the earth until the man was made, or just before he was made. Again, this leads right back to a very short period for creation. Rather than leaving the scientist "free of [B]iblical constraints in hypothesizing about cosmic origins," Genesis 2:5 appears to put some rather serious constraints on him.

Given the blatant paradoxes in Kline's thinking, it is amazing his work even made it into print, let alone became as influential as it has been. However, such is the uncritical climate in which we live. An innovator can easily gain the ear of those sympathetic to his agenda.

Can a literal, seven-day creation be reconciled with Genesis 2:5 without appearing ridiculous? That is not so difficult as Kline would have his readers believe. First of all, the King James Version does not press the causal relationship as hard as the American Standard which Kline insists upon. Secondly, Genesis 2:4 predicates the rest of the chapter (and indeed, everything through the end of chapter 4) as being about the "generations of the heavens and the earth." Everywhere else "these are the generations" is used, one finds genealogies. For example, Genesis 5 is about the "generations of Adam" and Genesis 10 is about the "generations of Noah."

The question is, what are the generations of the heavens and the earth? Genesis 2:5 tells the reader plainly: vegetation and man.[19] The next few verses tell how they came to be, as a product of heaven and earth.

God watered the earth so it would bear fruit. God made man from the earth and breathed life into him. The rest of Genesis 2-4 further explains the relationship of the man and the ground. The man sinned and the ground was cursed. The man spilled his brother's blood and the ground refused to yield its strength to him.

Thus Genesis 2:4ff. is plainly not a step-by-step chronological account of creation (as Genesis 1 so plainly is) but a genealogical account. Thus, verses 5-7 go straight from vegetation to man, not because the animals didn't come in between chronologically, but because the two generational lines of heaven and earth were specially interdependent. Man needs the vegetation to eat, and the vegetation needs man to cultivate it. Likewise, Genesis 2:5 mentions rainfall because, even if God had abundantly planted the earth, watering was necessary for the earth to bring forth succeeding generations of fruit. In conclusion, there is no conflict between a young earth and Genesis 2:5, as Kline insists.

THE DANGER OF THE DECONSTRUCTIONISTS

The truth is, deconstructionists always run into trouble when they try to interpret Genesis 1 away. In the end, the result is uniformly to promote atheism and unbelief, while diminishing God, God's law-word, and the redemptive work of Jesus Christ. Such deconstructionists are much more dangerous than the ingenuous atheist-scientist, just as poisoned food is much more dangerous than a bottle of poison labeled as such.

REFERENCES

1 Karl Popper originated the idea that a statement must be falsifiable to have scientific content.
2 Mark Ludwig, *Computer Viruses, Artificial Life and Evolution* (American Eagle Publications, 1993).

3 The author, Robert Chambers, revealed his identity years later. He was a respectable Edinburgh businessman.

4 *The Witness* was the official organ of the evangelical secessionist branch of the Church of Scotland.

5 Hugh Miller, *The Old Red Sandstone* (1841) in *Collected Works* (1869).

6 Saint Georges Mivart, *The Genesis of Species* (1871), 279.

7 James McCosh, *Christianity and Positivism* (1871), 37. See also his article "On Evolution" in J. G. Wood, *Bible Animals* (1877).

8 R. A. Torrey, *What the Bible Teaches* (1898), 249.

9 Augustus Strong, *Systematic Theology*, viii.

10 B. B. Warfield, *Biblical and Theological Studies* (1911), 238.

11 *The Fundamentals* IV, 91-104.

12 Marilyn Ferguson, *The Aquarian Conspiracy* (1980), 50.

13 Teilhard de Chardin, *The Heart of the Matter* (1979), 92.

14 Meredith G. Kline, "Space and Time in the Genesis Cosmogony," Perspectives *in Science and the Christian Faith*, March, 1996.

15 Notably, H. Blocher, *In the Beginning* (1984), C. E. Hummel, *The Galileo Connection* (1986) and R. Maatman, *The Impact of Evolutionary Theory: A Christian View* (1993).

16 Kline insists that the ASV is superior to the KJV because of its translation of the word *terem* as "not yet" rather than "before." Kline claims that translating *terem* as "before" is to "muff" the translation, which simply is not true.

17 Meredith G. Kline, "Because It Had Not Rained," *The Westminster Theological Journal* 20 (1958), 146-157.

18 A third option is possible, albeit intellectually dishonest in the face of Kline's goal of relieving the scientist of Biblical constraints. That would be to deceitfully distance the idea of "ordinary providence" from physical process. The reasoning would be something like this: since there were no plants, no rain was necessary, ergo the ordinary providence of watering plants by way of evaporation and rainfall was unnecessary; hence, the laws which cause evaporation would be unnecessary and therefore inoperative. This would suggest a world where normal physical processes were not operative at all, but they would not violate Kline's thesis because non-operative laws did not contribute to or detract from God's provision for living things.

19 The obvious connection is lost in translation. The original Hebrew says there was "no adam (man) to till the adamah (ground)" making the connection between the ground and the man obvious.

→ Chapter 5 ←

THE DOCTRINE OF
CREATION AND CHRISTIAN APOLOGETICS
by Cornelius Van Til

hen the apostle Paul preached to the Athenians on Mars Hill, he challenged them to become Creator-worshippers, instead of creature-worshippers (*Ac. 17*). It is this that all other believers, since the time of Paul, have also done. To realize why Paul did this, we must go back to Adam.

Adam disobeyed the command of God with respect to the tree of the knowledge of good and evil; he became a creature-worshipper instead of a Creator-worshipper. He declared his independence from God. He did not want God to tell him who he was and what he should do. Adam tried to shake off that which Satan had told him was an unwholesome and unbearable harness placed on him by "God." He wanted to be his own law-giver (autonomy).

To escape the punishment God had said would follow upon his disobedience to God, Adam sought to make himself believe that the world is not under God's control at all, that is, that God did not create the world and that therefore He cannot control it. Adam tried to make himself believe that Satan was right when he said that God was Himself only a part or aspect of the world. If you are to be really free, that is, independent of God, Satan suggested to Adam, you must think of the whole world, including God, as having come into existence by chance. Then everybody has equal rights and an equal chance to make his own fortune.

The result of Adam's choice actually meant slavery and death, not only for himself, but also for all his descendants. All men, Paul tells us, have sinned in Adam (*Rom. 5:12*). All men are fallen (apostate) in and with him. All men in Adam have adopted Satan's hypothesis about man and his world. All men are, therefore, subject to the wrath of God.

All men know that they are created by God and that, therefore, Satan was wrong in what he told Adam (*Rom. 1*). All men are like the prodigal son in the parable of Jesus. The prodigal knew that he was the son of his father. He knew that the change he jingled in his pocket had come from the father. But he had pasted a mask on his face which no one, not even he himself, was able to remove. He made himself and others believe that all his wealth came from his own gold mines. Where were those gold mines? He did not know. The only thing he "knew" was that they *did not* belong to his father. The prodigal hated the father and the father's house. It was this hatred of his father that controlled his view of the world. Only God's grace could unpaste the mask, the mask which had only anti-father lenses cemented in the eyeholes.

THE GREEKS AS FOLLOWERS OF SATAN

The Greeks to whom Paul preached exhibited the same attitude that Adam, after he listened to Satan, displayed. The Greeks did not prove; they could not prove; they just assumed that they were not image-bearers of God and that the universe about them was not created by God at all, but was "just there."

The Greeks simply assumed: (a) that all things are at bottom One, (b) that infinite plurality of things they saw in the space-time world about them eternally ooze out of this One, and (c) that this same plurality is also from all eternity being reabsorbed into this One. Thales said that *All* is water. Anaximander said that *All* is indefinite. Anaximanes said that *All* is Air. Parmenides said that *All* is static, and Heraclitus said that *All* is flux. The important point here is not the differences among them as to the nature of the *All* but the fact that all of them said that *all* reality is of one substance.

They all assumed that God's being is not different from man's being and that man's being is not different from God's being. They all assumed that there has not been a creation out of nothing at the beginning of time. This is the philosophy of *monism*.

To say what Paul said, that God is the self-sufficient Triune Being and that man's existence is derivative because this God had created him "out of nothing," that is, by mere expression of His will, was nonsense to the Greeks.

PARMENIDES AND PAUL

Parmenides expressed that attitude of all the Greeks in his classic phrase to the effect that "Being and Thought are Identical" because they *must* be identical. Only that which I can think without contradiction, said Parmenides, can exist; creation out-of-nothing is against the law of contradiction and therefore impossible. Man's autonomous mind is therefore the ultimate standard of reality.

We can imagine Paul and Parmenides having a quiet talk one evening. They would not have argued about details. Neither of them would have argued that his position is more "in accord with logic" and/or more "in accord with fact" than that of the either. Each would have claimed that only his position, rather than that of the other, was "thinkable" at all. Spinoza said in effect what Parmenides has said: "The order and connection of things is identical with the order and connection of ideas." We may put the matter in more modern terms. Parmenides and Spinoza might have said that only on the presupposition that all reality *is*, in Parmenides' sense of the term, can anything intelligible be said about anything. Man's mind *must* conform to the reality that *is*, by definition — man's definition.

CREATION AND THE PHILOSOPHY OF HISTORY

To make this point clear, we must understand that for Paul the idea of creation was but the beginning of a philosophy of history. This philosophy includes such teaching as the resurrection of Christ and His return from heaven to judge the living, and judging according as they have or have not accepted Christ as their king before their death. Moreover, the notion of creation as an aspect of this view of reality as a whole is taken from the Scriptures of the Old and New Testaments as the word of the Christ Who identified Himself as the way, the truth, and the life (*Jn. 14:6*). Paul *proclaims* his philosophy of history to the Greeks, in the name of and by the absolute authority of Jesus, the Christ Who had appeared to him from heaven on his way to Damascus, where he intended to destroy those who were of that *Way*, the Way of Jesus Christ. "Saul, Saul, why persecutest thou me?" Jesus had said to him. In other words, "Why have you repressed the Truth speaking to you in nature, in your conscience, and in the Scriptures?"

From this time forth, Paul preached Christ, Whom before he had persecuted, as the only light and life of men. All men, he said, are spiritually dead; without the life-giving power of the Holy Spirit, Who takes the things of Christ and gives them unto men, they keep going down the staircase that ends in eternal futility — intellectually, morally, and spiritually — until they join Satan in eternal separation from the God of love. "Hath not God made foolish the wisdom of the world, for after that the world by wisdom knew not God it pleased God through the foolishness of preaching to save those that believe" (*1 Cor. 1:20-21*).

"Parmenides, my friend," Paul might have said, "you have assumed that you are not created but ultimate, and that your thought is not that of a creature but instead is creative or legislative in the way that God's thought is creative and legislative. We both have pre-interpreted 'fact' and 'logic' in terms of our comprehensive and mutually exclusive views. I once held to a view basically similar to yours. I now see that 'logic' and 'fact' must be what alone they can be according to the 'gospel' of creation and redemption in Christ. They *are* because they must be *what they are said to be* in the total configuration of history, from creation to judgment portrayed in Scripture, and what I now, in the name of Christ, declare them to be. Having seen this, I no longer do what I formerly did, that is, try to penetrate exhaustively the relation of the Triune Creator-Redeemer God to myself and the created; I merely seek to make as much order as I can relating the facts of the space-time cosmos to one another and to God, thus forming a 'system' of knowledge. I am always mindful that this 'system' of mine is true because it is based on God's revelation to me in Christ, but it nevertheless remains subject to further development because I am only a creature using the laws of the Creator. My thinking is not originally constructive but recreatively reconstructive of the revelation of God."

PLATO AND PAUL

The principle of Parmenides has been called "the adequacy of thought to begin." It affirms the capacity of man's mind to comprehend the universe. Plato used this principle in his philosophy. But in his later life, he realized that he could not think through the space-time world exhaustively by means of his power of conceptualization. In his later dialogues, Plato's *non-being* of his earlier dialogues changed into *"otherness of being."* In the *Timaeus* dialogue, this "otherness of being" appears as an anti-being — a restraining force to the effort of the demiurge to make a perfect world. How can the best of sculptors make a perfect statute if the marble he has to work with is marred? Plato's "creator" was not omnipotent. The "stuff" of existence — matter — endlessly resists the "efforts" of impersonal forms to shape it.

Paul's gospel of any original, perfect man, who had disobeyed the known will of God, and as such was subject to the wrath of God, could not be conjoined with the life and worldview of Plato. Paul challenged the Greeks to reject their satanically inspired impersonal form-matter scheme as being internally meaningless and hateful in the sight of their Creator to Whom they owed allegiance.

PLOTINUS

Plotinus developed this form-matter scheme of the Greeks into his notion of the *scale of being*. In this scale of being, Plotinus has room for everything except for the Creator-Redeemer God of Scripture. In the philosophy of Plotinus, the Greek apostate, the spirit — the Greek *paideia* — challenges to a duel the Biblical scheme of creation, fall, and redemption through Christ. The concept of some universal scale of being that fuses God's being to the creation's being is a monistic concept — the heritage of Adam's rebellion. God becomes merely one aspect of being in general: crucial, but not *that* crucial! This was the intellectual challenge of Plotinus, the Greek.

AUGUSTINE

Augustine accepted this challenge. As Paul had been changed by the grace of Christ from being a persecutor of Jesus to His greatest apostle, so Augustine gradually emerged from the disfiguring detritus of Platonism and of Greek philosophy to the glorious vision of his creation and redemption by the Triune God of the Scriptures. The Creator is also the Savior.

In his later writings, Augustine worked out the implications of the Biblical teaching on creation by opposing the self-salvation idea in the Greek notion of man as inherently participant in God. This Greek notion had been insinuated into the Christian church by such men as Pelagius. For a brief time, Augustine won the day. But at an evil hour Pseudo-Dionysius and John Scotus Erigena brought back the Plotinian scale of being idea into the church. They did so by allegorizing the creation narrative. Before them Plato had already spoken of creation as a myth. If creation is mythical, God is mythical.

THOMAS AQUINAS

Following in this line of thinking the medieval theologians, and notably Thomas Aquinas, accommodated the Biblical idea of creation to the Greek idea of slenderness of being. Man is free because he has being, but only a little being. Following the Greeks, and more particularly Aristotle, "the Philosopher," the Council of Trent rejected Protestant theology as heresy, since Protestantism is grounded in the idea of man's freedom as that of the creature of the Triune God, accomplishing his task as a prophet, priest, and king unto God. The theology of the Reformation, based on the simple teaching of Paul about creation, sin, and redemption, was anathematized as heretical in the name of a Christianized Greek philosophy. (The attempt by Roman Catholic scholars such as Hans Küng and their Protestant counterparts to minimize the differences between the Council of Trent and Protestantism is grounded on a modernized, Kantian reinterpretation of Christian categories and language.)

IMMANUEL KANT

In modern times, Immanuel Kant developed the satanic notion of human autonomy more consistently than anyone before him.

On the surface, Kant's position is quite diverse from that of Parmenides and Plato. Whereas for Parmenides reality — *true* reality — is exhaustively eternal, for Kant it is exhaustively temporal. Even so, as Parmenides needed the idea of ultimate contingency as a foil to his notion of utterly timeless being, so Kant needed the idea of timeless logic and as a foil to his notion of time or contingency.

All apostate philosophy is constituted by correlative interaction between rationalist-determinism and irrationalist-indeterminism. Such philosophies are based on the notion of human autonomy. What Herman Dooyeweerd calls the "freedom-nature" scheme of post-Kantian thought and what he calls the "form-matter" scheme of Greek thought are but two forms of apostate thought, and both are *dialectical*.[1] Modern thought merely works out the implication of Greek thought to the effect that (a) all reality is at bottom One, (b) all temporal reality is working itself back into the One, that is, the notion that God and man develop together as aspects of one being. In the place of the Biblical idea of God as Creator and man as His creature, all apostate thinking has equally ultimate forces of form and matter eternally striving against one another.

RECENT EVOLUTIONARY THINKING

In recent times, evolutionary thinking has carried on the apostate man's notion that all being is one. Working along the lines of Kant, recent science, recent philosophy, and recent theology have taken for granted that there is not and cannot be any such thing as creation out of nothing.

When in 1859 Charles Darwin published his *Origin of Species*, he thought he was "proving" that man has come from an animal ancestry by self-existent cosmic forces. The evolution hypothesis in science involves the idea of cosmic evolution. Cosmic evolution, which Kant argued for a century before Darwin, necessarily preceded "scientific" evolution. There is no possibility of carrying to a conclusion an argument between those who believe in biological evolution and those who believe in creation, unless this argument be seen to be but an aspect of two mutually exclusive views of reality as a whole.

Modern biological evolution theory *assumes* that all reality is flux. It does this together with modern science in general.

It might appear that in modern evolutionary thinking, Heraclitus' idea that *all is flux* has won out over
the Parmenidean idea that *all is static*. Yet no one can
say anything about "all being as flux." How can a white-
cap on a bottomless and shoreless ocean of chance
say, *"Here I am"*? There is no possibility of man iden-
tifying either himself or any fact in his environment in
a universe of *pure* chance. As long as he holds that all
is flux, he cannot even get under way to ask a question
about *anything*, let alone giving any answers to any
questions he might ask.

Yet the modern scientist simply asserts or assumes
that there cannot be any such thing as creation out of
nothing, and he ignores the consequences of what his
denial entails for the question of the philosophy of history. In other words, modern science stands on the
surface of a bottomless ocean of chance as it announces
that Christianity *cannot* be true. The Heraclitean idea
of all reality as being *pure flux* needs the support of the
Parmenidean idea of all reality as *purely static* in order
to justify "autonomous" science's assumption that creation cannot have taken place in the past and that
there cannot be any such thing as a coming judgment
by Christ, in and by Whom all things are and were
created (*Rev. 4:11*).

When Darwin's theory of evolution was first presented, there was great rejoicing among those who were
anxious to see the historic Christian faith discredited.
At last it had been "proved" by the "facts" that man
had not been created by the self-sufficient God of the
Scriptures. By now it should be clear for all to see that
the very idea of space-time fact is utterly unintelligible
on the basis of reality as total flux. By now it should
also be clear that a combination of the idea of pure
irrationalist indeterminism and the idea of pure ratio-
nalist determinism is meaningless. A great philosopher
of science, Morris Cohen, says that science needs the
idea of a universe that is both *wholly* closed and *wholly*
open. This idea of the *pure correlativity* of pure staticism

and pure flux underlies all modern evolutionary science. No one could say anything intelligible on such a foundation.

MODERN PHILOSOPHY

We have come from the philosophy of Kant, with its notion that *time* or chance is ultimate, to the idea of science built on chance. We must turn for a moment to a brief look at the philosophical positions developed by men who lived after biological evolution had been "discovered."

In his book on *The Limitations of Science*, J. W. N. Sullivan writes that "we shall never reach a set of concepts in terms of which all the phenomena can be described. The entities used in science are abstractions from experience" (p. 105). In other words, according to Sullivan, the pure fluidity of chance must be frozen by the pure conceptual determinism of pure staticism. In order to have science at all, purely fluid sense-experience must be, yet cannot be, exhaustively expressed by an abstract, timeless conceptualization process. And when the "facts" are thus discovered and seen for what they really are, they are seen as never having been originated and as never possibly coming to be. Thus, a pure dualism between conceptualization and sensuous experience is turned into a monism of pure negation: no past or future is allowed.

A. N. Whitehead's philosophy is often called a process-philosophy. Whitehead rejects the older static views of science. He aims to develop a "higher concept" of science, a concept that will include the notion of human freedom as well as of impersonal necessity. "We must start," says Whitehead, "with the event as the ultimate unit of natural occurrence."[2] Taking the idea of the event "as a process whose outcome is a unit of experience" enables Whitehead, as he thinks, to enthrone freedom above all forms of necessity that one might find in reality.

The idea of event as a "unit of experience" also enables Whitehead to avoid paying "metaphysical compliments" to God.[3] As with Kant, Whitehead makes room for faith, that is, for *a faith other than the historic Christian faith*. The historic Christian faith would, argues Whitehead, be deterministic. True religion is, for Whitehead, "the vision of something which stands beyond, behind, and within, the passing flux of immediate things; something which is real, and yet waiting to be realized; something which is a remote possibility, and yet the greatest of present facts; something that gives meaning to all that passes, and yet eludes apprehension; something whose possession is the final good, and yet is beyond all reach; something which is the ultimate ideal, and the hopeless quest."[4]

MODERN THEOLOGY

Modern theology as well as modern philosophy agrees with modern science in building its structure on the assumption that historic reality is not created by the self-sufficient, self-contained Triune God of Scripture.

The prince of modern theologians is Karl Barth. His entire philosophy is built on the assumption that the Genesis account of the origin of man and his world must be allegorized. To be sure, Barth insists that theology needs the idea of creation. Creation is the foundation of the covenant, and the covenant is the essence of the relation of God to man. God *is* Christ, and Christ is His work of the saving of all men. There are *not* two natures, the divine and the human, that are genuinely united in Christ but without mixture. That was the Confession of Chalcedon. But we must "actualize Chalcedon." We must say that it is God's very nature to turn into the opposite of Himself and then take all men back up into participation with His own self-existence. "In Jesus Christ it comes about that God takes time to Himself; that He Himself becomes temporal; that He is present for us in the form of our own existence and our own world, not simply embracing our time and ruling it, but submitting Himself to it, and permitting created time to become and to be the form of His eternity."[5]

THE KINGDOM OF MAN

It is thus that modern process theology, building on modern process philosophy and modern process science, is leading men into the "dust of death." Senior demon Screwtape, in his second letter to his nephew Wormwood, points out that "one of our great allies at present is the Church itself." Not the invisible church, but the "sham Gothic" building and its ordinary looking members. He might also have included its "sham orthodoxy."

Jesus said that the last days would be like those of the time of Noah. Long before Socrates came upon the scene, Lamech scorned the idea that he was guilty because he was breaking the ordinances of God, especially the ordinance of monogamous marriage. And the children of Seth had joined the children of Cain in rejecting the creation-ordinances of God.

So now, as Jesus predicted, leading theologians are led by leading philosophers and scientists in assuming that there cannot be any such thing as a clear and finished revelation of God to man in history. Leading theologians are saying, "Lo here is Christ, or there" (*Mt. 24:23*). Believers in Christ now see the modern equivalent of the "abomination of desolation, spoken of by Daniel the prophet, standing in the holy place" (*Mt. 24:15*).

The main target of attack on the part of the theologians of the kingdom of man is the traditional Protestant view of Scripture and its content. It is the "literalism" of and the "determinism" of the Reformers and their followers that the "free man" of modern apostate thinking cannot tolerate. Just as Dionysius the Aereopagite and John Scotus Erigena allegorized the entire narrative of Scripture in terms of the flux theory of reality, so men like Paul Tillich have in our day mythologized the creation story and all that goes with it. To be sure, Tillich speaks of a final revelation in Jesus Christ. But, for Tillich, revelation is final only "if it has the power of negating itself without losing itself."[6] His thought, like that of the Greeks, is dialectical.

In Tillich's view, "Adam" was quite right in following Satan's advice to seek for freedom independently of the creation-redemption ordinances of God. Orthodox literalism is absurd. We must seek for a "cosmic myth" behind the Genesis story. This myth probably has "Orphic roots....It received a Christian form by Origen, a humanistic one by Kant, and is present in many other philosophies and theologies of the Christian Era. All have recognized that existence cannot be derived from within existence, that it cannot be derived from an individual event in time and space. They have recognized that existence has universal dimension."[7]

As for modern Roman Catholic theology, can one think of it as lagging behind in adopting the idea of biological and cosmic evolution? The great scientist-theologian Teilhard de Chardin tells the story of the emergence of Christ from the amoebae with great enthusiasm. How glorious the process of final victory of man over nature and over himself is now seen to be![8]

As for Roman Catholic philosophy, we may take Jacques Maritan as an illustration. Maritan too speaks of the great freedom that man has in terms of the *Philosophia Perrennis*. This philosophy is bound to be the philosophy of the future. It has taken into its bosom all the progress made by modern evolutionary scientific thought, while yet it holds to the permanence imbedded in Aristotle's thinking. The "Christian Aristotelianism of Albert the Great and particularly of St. Thomas Aquinas" offers us a truly "objective outlook on reality, and, at the same time looks upward in accordance with the theology of the church."[9] Such theologians as Hans Küng and Yves Congar take a position similar to that of Maritan.

Vatican II has followed the lead of these and similar theologians of flux. Its notorious assertion to the effect that there is no salvation outside the church (*extra ecclesia nulla salus*) is no barrier to the idea of universal salvation. The "church" now includes all men of good will.

Thus we find that leading Protestant theologians and leading Roman Catholic theologians join hands in terms of modern evolutionary thinking. But the end is not yet. The Master Historian of World History, Arnold J. Toynbee (cf. vol. 27 of *Wisdom*) invites us to see that Christianity and all other higher religions "have addressed themselves to Humanity in general in an *élan* of love."[10] In the course of biological cosmic evolution, creative personalities have sprung forth who have sought to transfigure their fellow men into living in accord with the "law of love."[11]

Jesus was one of these creative personalities: Buddha was another. Jesus exhibited the cosmic principle already expressed by Aeschylus, to the effect that all suffering sanctifies. Toynbee makes certain that no one who makes special redemptive claims for Jesus should be allowed citizenship in the universal kingdom of man. The historian "will be suspicious *a priori*," says Toynbee, "of any presentation that goes on to assert that a *unique* and *final* revelation has been given by God to *my* people in *my* time on *my* satellite of *my* sun in *my* galaxy. In this self-centered application of the thesis that God reveals Himself to His creatures the historian will espy the Devil's cloven hoof."[12]

THE CHRISTIAN'S ANSWER

This may suffice to indicate the fact that evolutionary philosophy is generally accepted by leading scholars in all fields of inquiry today. This may also suffice to indicate that the acceptance of the notion of evolution as a substitute for that of creation in the Biblical meaning of the term is not something to which open-minded men were led by the evidence of fact and the probative force of logic. On the contrary, the evolution doctrine is accepted in spite of the fact that it is inherently destructive of the possibility of all meaningful human speech and action. The evolution hypothesis is a view of reality by which the natural man, following Adam, seeks freedom from the laws of his Creator-God, and is caught in the dialectical net of having to interpret himself and his world in terms of the interaction between pure impersonal rationalistic determinism and pure impersonal irrationalistic indeterminism. This philosophy shows men's hatred of the God Who is understood, deep in the heart of each man, to be the Creator. This hatred makes men cling, in defiance to God's revelation, to a worse-than-meaningless view of themselves and the world.

What, then, are Christian believers to do in this situation? They are not to seek to answer evolutionary theory by means of a theology or philosophy that is itself based in part on the same false idea of "human freedom as autonomy" that underlies the evolution view. This excludes the use of Roman scholasticism or neo-scholasticism, for both are largely built upon the Aristotelian notion of the *analogy of being*, and this notion ultimately rests on the impossible correlativity of pure Parmenidean staticism and pure Heraclitean flux.[13] The analogy of being seeks to supply the "objectivity" that man needs for this thought by means of the notion of "being" inherent in the consciousness of man.

In the second place, it is equally impossible to reply successfully to evolutionary thinking by means of Protestantism's traditional Butler-analogy method of apologetics, with its supposedly logical proofs of God.[14] Furthermore, there is no hope in the concept of objectivity offered by the evangelical thinker C. S. Lewis — the notion of a universal *Tao* (way) taught by all higher religions.[15] This *Tao* is itself a projection of the would-

be-autonomous man as he emerges from his hypothetical animal life to his equally hypothetical divinity.

The only way in which evolutionary thinking can
be answered is by following the method of the Apostle
Paul. Paul tells apostate man that all the facts of the
entire world of space and time clearly manifest the creative, controlling, redeeming work of God. Paul tells
apostate man that his attempt to interpret the world
in terms of himself as "free" from God is clearly the
effort of one who is involved in the fall of Adam, and
represents the same sort of hostility to God that Adam
manifested when he listened to Satan. Accordingly,
apostate man's activity of thought and behavior is not
only futile but God-insulting. Accordingly, the wrath
of God rests and will rest forever upon the "children of
disobedience" unless they repent and believe in Christ
and His resurrection.

Paul tells apostate man that he himself is not in
himself any wiser or better than they. He has been
taken out of the depth of intellectual chaos and moral
corruption by the substitutionary death for him by
Christ on the cross and by the application of the significance of this death for him by the regenerating and
enlightening work of the Holy Spirit.

Such being the case, says Paul, "I now see that the
facts and the laws of the created universe in relation to
one another are what they are because of God's purpose in creating and redeeming a people for Himself
which should proclaim His praise. Only if man takes
his interpretative efforts to be that of reinterpretation
(as a redeemed creature) of God's original interpretation — given to him in Christ — as the way, the truth,
and the life, will he have light and freedom."

If the Christian is deeply convinced that he himself
was formerly caught in the clutches of the god of this
world, he will speak with deep sympathy to those who
are "outside" the freedom with which Christ has made
them. "Your freedom," he will say to his friend, "is, in
reality, nothing but slavery. Flee to Christ for true

freedom. Pray to the Holy Spirit to enable you to repent and believe.

"Yes, to say this is apparently contradictory. But the only alternative to it is freedom in a vacuum and the wrath of God remaining upon you."

REFERENCES

1 Herman Dooyeweerd, *In the Twilight of Western Thought* (n. p., 1960), chap. 2.
2 A. N. Whitehead, *Science and the Modern World* (n. p., 1925), 103.
3 *ibid.*, 179.
4 *ibid.*, 191.
5 Karl Barth, *Kirchliche Dogmatik II*, ii, 694, Eng. Tr. 616.
6 Paul Tillich, *Systematic Theology I* (n. p., n. d.) 148.
7 *ibid.*, II, 40, 41.
8 cf., C. Van Til's study, *Pierre Teilhard de Chardin.*
9 John S. Zybura, ed., *Present Day Thinking and the New Scholasticism* (n. p., 1926), 402.
10 Arnold J. Toynbee, *A Study in History, III* (n. p., n. d.) 232.
11 *ibid.*, 236.
12 _____, *An Historian's Approach to Religion* (n. p., n. d.) 135.
13 cf. C. Van Til. "Analogia Entis," in Edwin Palmer, ed., *The Encyclopedia of Christianity I*, (n. p., n. d.), 200-201.
14 cf. C. Van Til, *The Defense of the Faith* (n. p., 1963).
15 C. S. Lewis, *The Abolition of Man* (n. p., 1947).

✣ Chapter 6 ✣

REFORMED THEOLOGY
AND SIX-DAY CREATION

By Kenneth L. Gentry, Jr.

*A*s Reformed Christians we have a special stake in the creation/evolution debate. With our high view of Scripture, we are pre-committed to the integrity of the Word of God in all areas of life. Unfortunately, much of Reformed theology writes off six-day creation as naive fundamentalism or gross bibliolatry. Though most Reformed scholars would decry evolutionism, they often capitulate to the evolutionary elite, being pressured to re-interpret Genesis in order to maintain academic credibility. This is a tragic surrender of orthodoxy to the reigning cultural mythology of our day: chance-oriented, naturalistic evolutionism.

In this article I will provide a summary of the evidence from Scripture and the Westminster Confession which demands a literal, six-day creation position for Reformed Christians who operate under the Westminster Standards. I will also incorporate some subsidiary themes illustrating the necessity of the standard historical-grammatical approach to Genesis. Let us begin with our confessional position.

THE LANGUAGE OF THE CONFESSION

Some Reformed Christians deny that God created the heavens and the earth in six literal days. This denial brings them into clear contradiction with the Westminster Standards, which teach that the Lord God created the heavens and the earth "in the space of six days" (WCF 4:1; LC #15, SC #9).

It is important to note that here the Confession is not merely picking up the language of Scripture and quoting it, thereby leaving the language open to interpretation. The six-day statement is not a catch phrase. The Assembly very clearly speaks of a literal, six-day creation, when it states in WCF 4:1: "It pleased God the Father, Son, and Holy Ghost, for the manifestation of the glory of His eternal power, wisdom, and goodness, in the beginning, to create, or make of nothing, the world, and all things therein whether visible or invisible, in the space of six days; and all very good." The phrase "in the space of" demonstrates their concern with the temporal time-frame of the creative process.

In so stating the matter, the Westminster divines picked up on the language of John Calvin, who held to a six-day creation: "For it is too violent a cavil to contend that Moses distributes the work which God perfected at once into six days, for the mere purpose of conveying instruction. Let us rather conclude that God himself took the space of six days, for the purpose of accommodating his works to the capacity of men."[1] Calvin clearly had in mind literal days, for he states on page 105 of his Genesis commentary: "I have said above, that six days were employed in the formation of the world; not that God, to whom one moment is as a thousand years, had need of this succession of time, but that he might engage us in the consideration of his works." The language of the Confession and the sentiment of the Westminster divines are so obvious that even detractors from six-day creation have admitted the meaning of the Confession. One such opponent of six-day creation, Edward D. Morris, writes: "But the language of the Confession, in the space of six days, must be interpreted literally, because this was the exact view pronounced by the Assembly."[2]

THE GRAVITY OF THE ISSUE
FOR PRESBYTERIANS

This is a serious matter for ministers in confessionally-based Presbyterian churches. The Confession of Faith is historically definitional of Presbyterianism, and must be approached seriously. Presbyterian ministers must "sincerely receive and adopt" the Westminster Standards in their solemn ordination vows. It is apparent that the order and structure of the Confession of Faith are such that foundational issues of major consequence are placed first. The Confession of Faith is not a haphazard collection of doctrinal maxims; neither is it a systematic theological approach to doctrine. Instead it has an essential overall harmony that proceeds along a clear line of development: it first lays down foundational matters, then builds upon those in a logical and coherent fashion. As Philip Schaff notes: "The Confession consists of thirty-three chapters, which cover, in natural order, all the leading articles of the Christian faith from the creation to the final judgment."[3]

William Hetherington's classic work on the Confession elaborates a little more fully:

> The first thing which must strike any thoughtful reader, after having carefully and studiously perused the Westminster Assembly's Confession of Faith, is the remarkable comprehensiveness and accuracy of its character, viewed as a systematic exhibition of divine truth, or what is termed a system of theology. In this respect it may be regarded as almost perfect, both in its arrangement and in its completeness. Even a single glance over its table of contents will show with what exquisite skill its arrangement proceeds, from the statement of first principles to the regular development and final consummation of the whole scheme of revealed truth.... Thus viewed, the Confession of Faith might be so connected with one aspect of Church history as to furnish, if not a text-book according to chronological arrangement, in studying the rise and refutation of heresies, yet a valuable arrangement of their relative importance, doc-

trinally considered.... A few remarks may be made with regard to the plan according to which the Confession is constructed. A Confession of Faith is simply a declaration of belief in religious truths, not scientifically discovered by man, but divinely revealed to man. While, therefore, there may fairly be a question whether a course of Systematic Theology should begin with disquisitions relative to the being and character of God, as revealed, or with an inquiry what Natural Theology can teach, proceeding thence to the doctrines of Revelation, there can be no question that a Confession of Faith in revealed religion ought to begin with that revelation itself. This is the plan adopted by the Westminster Confession. It begins with a chapter on the Holy Scriptures; then follow four chapters on the nature, decrees, and works of God in creation and providence: and these five chapters form a distinct division, systematically viewed, of the Confession.[4]

In other words, foundational to the "system of doctrine" contained in the Confession and "sincerely received and adopted" by elders in the Presbyterian Church in America (Book of Church Order 21-5, #2) are the first five chapters of the Confession. Note the foundational logic of the Confession: Chapter 1 secures for us the infallible means whereby we know God, His will, and ways, *i.e.,* through Scripture. May we deny that God speaks infallibly and inerrantly in Scripture? May we deny any of the sixty-six books of Scripture? This chapter establishes for us our ultimate authority for framing our system of doctrine: the Word of God contained in the Old and New Testaments. All else fails in our doctrinal system if this chapter is not true. Chapter 2 moves quite necessarily to the nature and being of the God Whom we worship and serve. Which elements of our statement regarding the being of Almighty God may we remove? He is our very reason for existence.

Indisputably Chapter 2 must also be foundational to the whole system of doctrine contained in the Confession. Chapter 3 flows quite logically into a consideration of the decrees of God, which explain, uphold, and direct the entire universe. The God Whom we worship and serve is a sovereign Who planned all things by His eternal decree. This sets Christianity against all forms of unbelief and establishes our reason for serving the Lord God: He is absolutely sovereign. It explains also the rationality, significance, and value of the universe as rooted in the eternal plan of God. Chapters 4 and 5 turn to consider the very creation of the entire universe and all of its elements and the actual outworking of the decree of God in providence. This is the arena in which man will live in the service of God: a God-created, God-governed universe. Nothing other than God Himself accounts for the existence and control of all reality. The stage is set for considering the following doctrinal formulations of our faith and practice in the world which God created and governs.

A denial of the Confessional position on creation is a denial of a foundational principle of the Confession and our "system of doctrine." The Presbyterian Church in America deems "the doctrine of creation" to be one of "the fundamentals of our standards" (M19GA 2:479, 481). Not only so, but this denial of six-day creation is also a capitulation to the most significant unbelieving opposition to Scripture and Christianity today, a secular, humanistic-based science that proceeds from a chance oriented universe by means of uniformitarian science (although some state that they do not hold to any form of evolutionary theory).

SCRIPTURE AND CREATION

Any attempt to deny a process of creation involving a series of successive divine fiats stretching out over a period of only six literal days is manifestly contrary to the plain, historical sense of Scripture. The Hebrew word *yom* ("day") in the Genesis 1 account of creation should be understood in a normal sense of a 24-hour period, for the following reasons:

(1) *Argument from primary meaning.* The preponderant usage of the word *yom* ("day") in the Old Testament is of a normal day as experienced regularly by man (though it may be limited to the hours of light, as per common understanding). The word occurs 1704 times in the Old Testament, the overwhelming majority of which have to do with the normal cycle of daily earth time. Preponderant usage of a term should be maintained in exegetical analysis unless contextual forces compel otherwise. This is particularly so in historical narrative. R. L. Dabney points out:

> The narrative seems historical, and not symbolical; and hence the strong initial presumption is, that all its parts are to be taken in their obvious sense.... It is freely admitted that the word day is often used in the Greek Scriptures as well as the Hebrew (as in our common speech) for an epoch, a season, a time. But yet, this use is confessedly derivative. The natural day is its literal and primary meaning. Now, it is apprehended that in construing any document, while we are ready to adopt, at the demand of the context, the derived or tropical meaning, we revert to the primary one, when no such demand exists in the context.[5]

(2) *Argument from explicit qualification.* Moses carefully qualifies each of the six creative days with the phraseology: "evening and morning." The qualification is a deliberate defining of the concept of day. Outside of Genesis 1 the words "evening" and "morning" occur together in thirty-seven verses. In each instance it speaks of a normal day. Examples from Moses include:

Exodus 18:13: "And so it was, on the next day, that Moses sat to judge the people; and the people stood before Moses from morning until evening."

Exodus 27:21: "In the tabernacle of meeting, out-side the veil which is before the Testimony, Aaron and his sons shall tend it from evening until morning be-fore the LORD." R. L. Dabney argues that this evidence alone should compel adoption of a literal-day view:

> The sacred writer seems to shut us up to the literal interpretation, by describing the day as composed of its natural parts, "morning and evening."... It is hard to see what a writer can mean, by naming evening and morning as mak-ing a first, or a second "day"; except that he meant us to understand that time which includes just one of each of these successive epochs: — one beginning of night, and one beginning of day. These gentlemen cannot construe the expression at all. The plain reader has no trouble with it. When we have had one evening and one morn-ing, we know we have just one civic day; for the intervening hours have made just that time.[6]

(3) *Argument from ordinal prefix.* In the 119 cases in Moses' writings where the Hebrew word *yom* stands in conjunction with a numerical adjective (first, second, third, etc.), it never means anything other than a literal day. The same is true of the 357 instances outside the Pentateuch, where numerical adjectives occur.

Examples include:

Leviticus 12:3: "And on the eighth day the flesh of his foreskin shall be circumcised."

Exodus 12:15: "Seven days you shall eat unleav-ened bread. On the first day you shall remove leaven from your houses. For whoever eats leavened bread from the first day until the seventh day, that person shall be cut off from Israel."

Exodus 24:16: "Now the glory of the LORD rested on Mount Sinai, and the cloud covered it six days. And on the seventh day He called to Moses out of the midst of the cloud."

The Genesis 1 account of creation consistently applies the ordinal prefix to the day descriptions, along with "evening and morning" qualifiers (*Gen. 1:5, 8, 13, 19, 23, 31*).

(4) *Argument from coherent usage.* The word *yom* is used of the creative days of four, five, and six, which occur after the creation of the sun, which was expressly designated to "rule" the day/night pattern (*Gen. 1:14*). The identical word (*yom*) and phraseology ("evening and morning," numerical adjectives) associated with days four through six are employed of days one through three, which compel us to understand those days as normal earth days.

(5) *Argument from divine exemplar.* In Exodus 20:9-11 (the Fourth Commandment) God specifically patterns man's work week after His own original creational work week. Man's work week is expressly tied to God's: "for in six days the Lord made heaven and earth" (*Ex. 20:11*). On two occasions in Moses' writings this rationale is used:

> Exodus 20:11: "For in six days the LORD made the heavens and the earth, the sea, and all that is in them, and rested the seventh day. Therefore the LORD blessed the Sabbath day and hallowed it."

> Exodus 31:15-17: "Work shall be done for six days, but the seventh is the Sabbath of rest, holy to the LORD.... It is a sign between Me and the children of Israel forever; for in six days the LORD made the heavens and the earth, and on the seventh day He rested and was refreshed."

Dabney's comments are helpful: "In Gen. ii:2, 3; Ex. xx:11, God's creating the world and its creatures in six days, and resting the seventh, is given as the ground of His sanctifying the Sabbath day. The latter is the natural day; why not the former? The evasions from this seem peculiarly weak."[7]

(6) *Argument from plural expression.* In Exodus 20:11 God's creation week is spoken of as involving "six days" (*yammim*), plural. In the 608 instances of the plural "days" in the Old Testament, we never find any other meaning than normal days. Ages are never expressed as *yammim.*

(7) *Argument from alternative idiom.* Had Moses intended to express the notion that the creation covered eras, he could have employed the term *olam.* Even the resting of God on the "seventh day" does not express His eternal rest, for it would also imply not only His continual rest but also His continual blessing of creation, as if sin never intervened: Genesis 2:3 — "Then God blessed the seventh day and sanctified it, because in it He rested from all His work which God had created and made."

THE UNIQUENESS OF THE CREATIVE FIATS

Our concern regarding this denial of six literal days also involves a contradiction with the Westminster Standards (WCF Chps. 4 & 5; LC #15 & 18, SC #9 & 11), due to a confusion of the theological concepts of creation and providence. Some argue that Genesis 1 suggests God frequently operated through protracted, providential governance in His creative work, rather than proceeding solely by a series of immediate, instantaneous fiat-acts. This is manifestly contrary to the revelation of God in Scripture, not only in Genesis 1, but elsewhere (*e.g., Ps. 33:9; Heb. 11:3*). This is a dangerous and unnecessary concession to modern secular-based science. It is not only an erroneous interpretation of the revelation of God, but provides a slippery slope to evolution, opening the doors to progressive creationism, threshold creationism, and, eventually, theistic evolution.

A common means of re-interpreting Genesis 1 is employing what is called the Framework Hypothesis. The Framework Hypothesis works on the assumption of a topical arrangement rather than a chronological arrangement of the material of Genesis 1. It suggests that obvious balance and parallel between Days 1-3 and Days 4-6 is clear evidence of the topical concerns of Moses. The proposed hypothetical, non-chronological framework for Genesis 1 fails structurally and logically. It possesses only an apparent and superficial parallelism, a parallelism that can be equally accounted for by the providential design of God in creation. Problems with the Framework Hypothesis abound. I will briefly mention just a couple. The Framework Hypothesis expressly and resolutely denies that Moses intended to provide a record of a sequence of chronological creational fiats and events, despite the wholesale structuring of Genesis 1 around a series of specifically enumerated days (first day, second day, etc.). This view argues rather that Moses merely provided a balanced artistic expression of the truth of divine creation *ex nihilo*, without providing any insight into God's *modus operandi* in creation. This dangerous hermeneutic methodology generates serious exegetical confusion regarding the proper approach to historical narrative in Scripture. This is amply illustrated in two main areas:

(1) Framework Hypothesists confidently interpret Genesis 1 artistically rather than chronologically. This interpretive procedure overthrows the obvious chronological development revealed in Genesis 1. It is a serious methodological flaw in this hermeneutic in that Genesis 1 provides both the revelational foundation to the universe and the world, as well as to the historical revelation of the development of the human race and of redemption in Genesis, which in turn is foundational to the theology and redemptive history of all of Scripture.

(2) Framework Hypothesists evidence exegetical and theological confusion by allowing that death in the sentiate animal kingdom (wherein resides the "breath of life" [e.g., *Gen. 6:17; 7:15, 22*]) was a part of the "very good" creation order as it originally came from the hand

of God (*Gen. 1:31*). That is, prior to the Fall of Adam and the resultant curse, death reigned. Confession and Scripture both concur that the befalling creation curse resulted in "the bondage of corruption" in "the creation itself" (*Rom. 8:21*) "which must be taken in the sense of the decay and death apparent even in non-rational creation."[8]

CONCLUSION

As Reformed Christians committed to the integrity of the inspired Word of God, we must hold to the teachings of Scripture, rather than the ever-changing doctrines of man. Genesis is foundational to the whole Bible; Genesis 1 is foundational to Genesis. The issues that hang in the balance are enormous. We should stand — in this area as in all others — with Paul and proclaim, "Let God be true, and every man a liar" (*Rom. 3:4*).

REFERENCES

1 John Calvin, "Genesis," Banner *of Truth* (1847 translation, 1965 publication), 78.

2 Edward D. Morris, *Theology of the Westminster Symbols*, (Columbus, OH, 1900), 202.

3 Philip Schaff, *The Creeds of Christendom* (Grand Rapids, 1990), 1:766.

4 William M. Hetherington, *History of the Westminster Assembly of Divines* (Edmonton, AB [1887], 1991), 350, 351, 357.

5 R. L. Dabney, *Lectures in Systematic Theology* (Grand Rapids [1878], 1972), 254-5.

6 *ibid.*, 255.

7 *ibid.*

8 John Murray, *Romans*, 1:304.

✣ Chapter 7 ✤

A CRITIQUE OF THE
FRAMEWORK HYPOTHESIS

By Frank Walker, Jr.

In 1985 the Eureka Classis of our denomination adopted two resolutions regarding the length of days in Genesis 1. The first sets forth the position of the Reformed Church in the United States (RCUS) on this issue: "The Eureka Classis affirms that God created the heavens and the earth in six normal days which were chronological periods of light and darkness as recorded in the book of Genesis."

A popular alternative to this traditional interpretation of the creation days is the framework hypothesis. Some of the ideas that eventually became part of this theory began to take form among liberal theologians in Germany in the middle of the last century, but Professor Arie Noordzij of the University of Utrecht first used it as an interpretive tool for Genesis 1 in 1924. Dr. Meredith G. Kline started teaching it at Westminster Theological Seminary (WTS) nearly half a century ago. Through him it has impacted the Presbyterian Church in America, the Orthodox Presbyterian Church, and other Reformed communions.

The second statement that the Eureka Classis adopted in 1985 addresses the framework view as it was being taught at Westminster. It reads, "That the Eureka Classis, Reformed Church in the United States, register a protest against the teaching at Westminster Theological Seminary in California and Philadelphia which questions the chronological sequence of the six normal days of light and darkness in Genesis 1. We believe that this skeptical interpretation of Holy Scripture is dangerous to the faith and theology of the students and to the churches which these students shall serve." Westminster Seminary in California responded with a letter of several pages. The Executive Committee then recommended, inasmuch as the two resolutions quoted above were adopted almost unanimously, that each Consistory write to Westminster to affirm our overwhelming agreement on this issue. Whether any Consistory did so is not stated in the record. The next year the representative of Westminster Seminary in California asked for time to address the Synod concerning this issue. Following this address, the Synod reaffirmed its commitment to the two resolutions of the previous year. Since that time, the Synod has neither amended nor rescinded its position.

A MATTER WORTH FIGHTING OVER

But is this something worth fighting for? The Southern California Presbytery of the OPC apparently does not think it is. In a debate over the licensure of a man who holds to the framework hypothesis, several commissioners said that they could not see any way that a person coming to Scripture with a Reformed hermeneutic could arrive at any conclusion other than six-day creation, but they did not want to make this a qualifying issue.

The RCUS takes a different view. The length of days is not really the issue. If God had wanted to make the entire universe in two seconds, He could have done so. Augustine thought it was even shorter than this. He could not imagine any reason why it would have taken an omnipotent God six days to do anything. Or if God had wanted to stretch out His creative activity to a hundred million years, that is also within the realm of His power. The issue at the heart of this controversy is not the length of days in Genesis 1, but one's view of Scripture. The approach of the Reformed church historically is grammatical and historical. Our goal is to interpret the statements of Scripture in their historical context. The framework hypothesis, on the other hand, relies to one degree or another on an additional element, namely, genre criticism. Because different rules apply to different genres of literature, the re-categorization of a piece of literature will necessarily cause its reader to ask a different set of questions. When a book begins with the words, "Once upon a time. . . ," we do not ask, "When did this take place?" We know that we are reading fiction and questions of history are irrelevant. But when a book begins, "The significance of Einstein's theory of relativity is . . . ," history, science, mathematics, philosophy, and a host of other subjects immediately raise their heads. The framework hypothesis removes Genesis 1 from history and reclassifies it as a poetic teaching device. The implication of this is that, although there are certain ideas in Genesis 1 that are historical (*e.g.,* the creation of the universe), the precise details (*e.g.,* chronology) need not be interpreted in a straightforward manner.

Recently, Mr. Futato of WTS (Escondido) wrote an article to supplement Kline's 1958 article. In this he uses genre criticism to turn the first chapter of Genesis into a polemic against Canaanite Baal worship. This is a reaction to the liberals who often claim that Genesis 1 is an adaptation of Baal mythology. His evidence for this is far from conclusive. Although it is well beyond the scope of this paper to evaluate his arguments, his paper shows how re-categorizing the genre of Genesis 1 changes the way we look at it.

The RCUS has considered the literary approach of genre criticism as well. In 1991 the Synod formed a committee to study the doctrine of Scripture as it is taught at WTS (Philadelphia). I was on that committee. My particular assignment was to study the views of Dr. Raymond Dillard. When I finished my report, I submitted it to Dr. Dillard to confirm that I had represented his views fairly and accurately; in fact, to be fair I purposely biased my report in his favor. Though I criticized his views, he admitted that my assessment of his teaching was correct. This report was presented to the RCUS Synod in 1995. I also wrote the conclusion, which begins, "Your committee concludes that there is a cause for concern about various forms of expression used by some professors at Westminster Seminary (Philadelphia), that, at the very least, obfuscate the historic, orthodox understanding of Scripture as defined by the Reformed creeds." The Synod adopted this report. Thus, ten years after defining its position on the days of creation, the Synod expressed its disapproval of the hermeneutical approach that allows one to hold to the framework hypothesis.

It has been said that six-day creation is a test of orthodoxy in the RCUS. This does not mean that we condemn or approve the whole of a man's theology solely on his view of creation, but that a man who holds to the day-age theory or the framework hypothesis holds to a view of creation unacceptable to the RCUS and is therefore ineligible for the office of elder or pastor.

Naturally, those who hold to other views want us to be more tolerant. They argue that the matter is not that clear, that it is a matter of interpretation. The fact is that every doctrine is a matter of interpretation, but this does not affect the fact that each church (denomination) has a God-given responsibility to determine which interpretation it believes to be the teaching of Scripture. We do this with Christology, theology proper, soteriology, and eschatology. By what logic, then, are we forbidden to adopt a standard concerning the doctrine of creation, especially if that standard is what the church has generally held down through the ages and is the most natural reading of the text?

THE FRAMEWORK HYPOTHESIS

The framework hypothesis holds that the "days" of creation have nothing to do with time, but are "forms" or "images" designed by God to help us understand creation. It is as if a person takes a trip across the United States. When he returns, he arranges his photographs by subject rather than in the order they were taken. Hence pictures of the Atlantic and Pacific Oceans are on one page, pictures of the Rockies and Appalachians on another, and the deserts of California and New Mexico on a third. Those who hold to the framework theory find it necessary to interpret Genesis 1 in this way because they believe that there are certain inconsistencies in Genesis 1 that compel a non-literal, non-chronological interpretation. Based on these supposed inconsistencies and the parallelism of the days, Genesis 1 is reclassified as a "literary device," "poetry," or "semi-poetic teaching device," from which we are to draw the conclusion that it cannot be accepted at face value as far as its chronology is concerned.

Here are some of the alleged inconsistencies noted by those who espouse the framework theory: (1) The sun was not created until Day Four *(vv. 14-19)*. Since the sun is the instrument used for measuring "days," there was no way to measure the first three days. How then are we to determine their length? (2) On the seventh day God rested from creation. He has not created anything since then, but has rather taken an eternal delight in His works (as we read in Hebrews 4). Thus, it is held, the seventh day is an eternal day and not a normal day. This at least leaves open the possibility that the other six days may be something other than normal days, too. But the greatest inconsistency, as the framework view holds it, is this: (3) Genesis 2:5, in describing Day Three, shows that God's *modus operandi* during the creation week was ordinary providence. Yet, if Day Three was a literal twenty-four hour day, this could not be, for it is impossible for all the water that covered the earth to have evaporated in that amount of time. However, the problem disappears if Day Three was longer than a normal day.

The poetic structure is fairly straightforward. It is as if there are two sets of days (Days One through Three and Days Four through Six). These two sets of days are actually describing the same creation-events. Days

One and Four are the same, as are Days Two and Five, and Days Three and Six:

Day 1 — light
Day 2 — separation of water and air
Day 3 — dry land and plants
Day 4 — light-bearers
Day 5 — birds and fish
Day 6 — inhabitants of dry land (animals, man)

Sometimes it is said that the first set of days portrays the spheres of creation and the second set the filling of the spheres. Others say that the first three days give the kingdoms and the second set the kings of the kingdoms. It would be hard to deny that there is some parallelism here. Is it not part of the beauty of creation?

EARLY CRITICISMS

Now, before we consider responses to these matters, there are a few things that I would like to say about the framework hypothesis in general.

First, how many theologians have studied the first two chapters of Genesis over the centuries and have never seen these inconsistencies to be of such a magnitude that they warrant a completely new theory of creation? For example, Calvin's comment on Genesis 2:5 shows an awareness of the problem mentioned earlier, but he offers an obvious solution: "But although he has before related that the herbs were created on the third day, yet it is not without reason that here again mention is made of them, in order that we may know that they were then produced, preserved, and propagated, in a manner different from that which we perceive at the present day." Here Calvin assumes that Genesis 2:5 is not a description of Day Three, for, though plants were certainly "produced"and "preserved"during the twenty-four hour period of Day

Three, which he firmly believed, it would be quite a stretch to say that they "propagated" in that time. In his commentary on Genesis 1, E. J. Young comes to the same conclusion and suggests that the framework theory crumbles when the assumption that Genesis 2:5 refers to Day Three is rejected. To the present writer's knowledge, this argument has never been satisfactorily answered.

Second, the framework approach causes problems for the doctrine of the perspicuity of Scripture. This doctrine says that the things necessary for our learning are so clearly revealed that even those of considerably diminished capacity can understand them well enough to be blessed by them. Of course, this does not mean that everything in the Bible is equally clear. If this were true, there would be no debate on many subjects. However, the doctrine of creation is essential for our understanding of origins, the person and work of Christ, regeneration, and the last things, to name a few; and it is referred to time and time again. It seems rather preposterous that only Jews of the fifteenth-century B. C. who may have been considering Canaanite Baal worship and twentieth-century theologians with an enlightened view of language have adequate knowledge to interpret Genesis 1 properly. The rest of the church throughout the ages has been hopelessly duped by the simple language of the narrative. Even Marcus Dods, a liberal Scottish theologian of the last century, agrees; he wrote, "If, for example, the word 'day' in these chapters does not mean a period of twenty-four hours, the interpretation of Scripture is hopeless."

And finally, there are no clear limits to the framework theory. If the so-called inconsistencies and literary devices warrant a reinterpretation of Genesis 1, why not do the same with Genesis 3? After all, if a talking serpent is not extraordinary, we would be hard pressed to find something that is. The same problem applies to the Flood and the tower of Babel. The miracles of Christ can be dismissed on the same basis. Young insists that even the resurrection of Christ cannot stand. In fact, this is exactly the approach that the liberals have taken. Once the door is opened, nothing holds together.

INCONSISTENCIES AND POETRY?

Now, let us move on to the "inconsistencies" mentioned earlier. I believe that their answers are fairly simple and straightforward. This is why theologians of previous eras were not bothered by them.

Can there be "time" without the sun? While it is true that the first three days had no sun, they were not without light (which was created on the first day) and this light, whatever its source may or may not have been (and certainly we believe that an omnipotent God can create light without a source of light), waxed and waned in periods of "evening and morning." If time is defined as the succession of events, as Augustine said, this certainly qualifies. By the repeated use of this phrase and the ordinals (first, second, third, etc.), the exegetical boundaries of the days of Genesis 1 are clearly defined. Elsewhere in Scripture, wherever both criteria are used, literal days are in view.

Even the length of the seventh day cannot be denied on the grounds that it was not described as "evening and morning." It differs qualitatively from the other six days, being a day of rest, not labor, and as such would allow an alternate closing. In fact, it seems that the early verses of Genesis 2 are just as definitive for the length of Day Seven as the other indicators are for the first six days. Notice, for example, that it is called the *seventh day* three times; that is, it is the seventh of whatever the first six were. If the first six days were normal days, the seventh day must be a normal day, too. This is especially so since by Day Seven the sun was in place and operating as the keeper of time. Thus, as far as creation was concerned, Day Seven was exactly twenty-four hours in duration.

As for Genesis 1 being poetry, it seems that there is an unspoken assumption that literary form and literal meaning are mutually exclusive. This, I believe, necessarily involves an incomplete and defective view of language. But why must we assume that poetry is literally false? Are the Psalms literally false simply because they employ Hebrew parallelism? If so, then every time a man writes a love poem to his sweetie he may actually be telling her how much he hates her. Likewise, the disjunction between literary form and literal chronology cannot be accepted without doing great harm to the Bible. Jean-Marc Berthoud, a Swiss Reformed scholar, says, "What difficulty would it be for [the Author of the Universe] to cause the most complex, refined literary form to coincide with the very way in which He Himself created all things in six days? Artistic form is in no sense opposed to an actual relation of facts, especially since the Author of the account is none less than the actual Creator of the facts which are described in that account...."

As a matter of fact, the parallelism of the creation narrative is not as exact as we are asked to believe. Again, Young deals with this in a rigorous argument covering several pages, but for our purposes I will quote just two paragraphs:

> Do the second and fifth days parallel one another? On day two there is a twofold fiat ("let there be a firmament ... and let it divide") and the fulfillment consists of two acts of God ("God made ... divided"), followed by a further act ("God called"). On the fifth day there is also a twofold fiat ("let the waters bring forth ... and the fowl let it fly") and then comes a fulfillment consisting of a threefold creative act of God ("God created ... great whales ... every living thing ... every winged fowl") and this is followed by two additional acts of God ("God saw ... God blessed"). As far as form is concerned, the parallelism is by no means exact.

Nor is there exact parallelism in content. The swarming waters and their inhabitants which were created in the fifth day are not to be identified with the primeval waters of day two. Rather, it is expressly stated that the fish are to fill the waters in the seas (verse 22), and the seas were brought into existence on the third day. For that matter, if a mere parallel with water is sought, we may note that "the waters" and the "abyss" are mentioned in verse two also.

In a footnote Young says that this is sufficient "to show that the alleged parallelism between days two and five is an illusion."At least it is not complete enough to warrant a theory based on it.

GENESIS 2:5

Since Genesis 2:5 is a pivotal passage for defenders of the framework hypothesis, I want to deal with it in greater detail. To repeat what we said earlier: the problem here is that Genesis 2:5 seems to conflict with Day Three. Day Three, if taken literally, pictures the drying up of the land at an abnormally rapid rate, but Genesis 2:5 suggests that God used processes of ordinary providence, including secondary causes (mist, rain, etc.), to make the world.

Mark Futato believes that Genesis 2:5-7 is a "logical, highly structured, and perfectly coherent" presentation of two problems, their reasons and their solutions. The problems are stated in the first half of verse 5: there was neither "wild vegetation"(*plant of the field*) nor "cultivated grain"(*herb of the field*) in the earth. The reasons why these two kinds of plants did not exist are given at the end of verse 5: there was no wild vegetation because *the LORD God had not caused it to rain upon the earth, and there was no cultivated grain because there was not a man to till the ground.* The solution to the lack of rain, which kept the wild vegetation from germinating, can be found in verse 6: God caused "rain clouds"(Futato's interpretation) to arise from the earth and water the whole ground. The absence of a cultivator is supplied in verse 7, where *the LORD God formed man of the dust of the ground*. He concludes that these normal processes (rain and human cultivation) were present during the time of creation since these verses describe the origin of certain plants. In a footnote, he specifically says that "other biblical accounts of creation [Ps. 104:13 and Prov. 3:19-20 in particular, but probably including Job 38-39] ... testify to the presence of rain from the beginning."

It seems that it is the concept of "other biblical accounts of creation" that causes the problem. The assumption seems to be that these other creation accounts diverge from each other so much that we must find a way to harmonize them. But a discrepancy appears only if we treat the other creation accounts as if they were independent of each other. In other words, we must assume the problem in order to find one. This is a clear case of *petitio principii* (begging the question). One would be hard pressed to find any indication of chronological sequence in the other so-called accounts; yet, this is exactly what Genesis 1 purports to offer. If only one account claims to be chronological, the difficulty vanishes.

All this is to say that Genesis 2:4ff. is not a second version of the creation narrative. The account of the creation of heaven and earth concludes with Genesis 2:3. Genesis 2:4 begins with the phrase, *"These are the generations."* Many years ago, Dr. Young demonstrated that this phrase, which occurs several times in Genesis, always introduces the results of the previous section. Thus, Genesis 2:4 introduces a new section that concentrates on one aspect of the completed creation, namely, the creation of man. It first considers the environment in which man would appear and then narrates the creation of man and his helper. Thus, Genesis 2:5 is not another explanation of Day Three, but a detailed description of an already created world with specific information relating to man's place in that world.

Genesis 2:5-7 anticipates the story that follows. Its function in the narrative is akin to the heading or sub-headings of a newspaper article. That is, they provide the basic story, but the details of that story come in what follows.

The plants mentioned in Genesis 2:5 are the same as those mentioned in Genesis 3:18. In fact, exactly the same words are used for *herb of the field*. Thus, Futato's definition of these plants as "wild vegetation" and "cultivated grain" is essentially correct. But what he misses is that neither of these kinds of plant life grew before the Fall exactly as they grew afterward. When Adam sinned, God cursed the entire world: *Thorns also and thistles shall it bring forth to thee; and thou shalt eat the herb of the field; in the sweat of thy face shalt thou eat bread (Gen. 3:18-19)*. Wild vegetation became a hindrance and an annoyance to man; God Himself would provide rain to cause it to flourish in man's world. Cultivated grain needed the tireless labor of a cultivator. Fallen man will eat only by the sweat of his brow. No more would Adam and Eve simply reach out their hands to eat the abundant fruit of the Garden of Eden. Genesis 2:5-7, then, helps the reader understand the drastic change that took place as a result of Adam's sin.

Earlier we said that Genesis 2:5 is not about Day Three. Now we see that there is no necessity to go in that direction; the reference to the absence of rain can be interpreted in another way that allows Genesis 1 to maintain its chronology. There is no need to interpret the days of Genesis 1 as anything other than days of normal duration as we know them today. In fact, Genesis 1 does not allow anything else.

Throughout Scripture, creation is spoken of as a six-day event. The clearest of these is the fourth commandment. When Moses gave the law to the Israelites, they knew what days were because they spent many of them out in the hot desert sun making bricks. The fourth commandment obligated them to follow the pattern for labor that God Himself established at the very beginning. Now, if the days of Genesis 1 are not the same kind of days that we know today, then this commandment makes no sense. "God put together six *images* of creation and then rested *forever*; therefore, we must work *six* days and rest one *day*"? This is called the fallacy of equivocation; that is, the meaning of the terms is not consistent throughout the argument.

Kline recognizes the force of this argument, though he obviously does not want to admit it or accept it. He says, "The argument that Genesis 1 must be strictly chronological because man's six days of labor follow one another in chronological succession forces the argument unnecessarily." He does not say why he thinks so, but continues, "The logic of such argument would not allow one to stop short of the conclusion that the creation 'days' must all have been of equal duration and twenty-four hours at that." So it does. Dr. Kline has unwillingly established our case.

This shows something else. Not only is the correct view of creation necessary for sound doctrine, but also for ethics. The framework hypothesis says that God structured the creation account with the six-to-one ratio to lay the groundwork for the fourth commandment to be given later. But if creation did not take place in six days, why did God find it necessary to make up a story to base the fourth commandment on? Could He not simply have given us the fourth commandment without a reason for it? What motivation is there to obey a God who manufactures reasons for our obedience?

✣ Chapter 8 ✣

LITERAL, SIX-DAY CREATION AND THE LOCAL CHURCH

By Charles A. McIlhenny

The focus of this article is on the work and discipline of the church, *i.e.*, the local congregation in relation to the six-day literal understanding of the creation account. The church's most celebrated day — the "marketplace of the soul," as the Puritans used to say — is the Lord's Day, and its worship is both public and private. The Christian Sabbath, the Lord's Day, belongs to the Lord of the Sabbath. And to speak of the literalness of the Sabbath day presupposes the literalness of the previous six days as well.

I take a literalist position on the creation account not because I like "literalism," nor because literalism is the only logical-rational defense against irrationalism, liberalism, and cultism; nor do I hold it for some unreasoning "fundamentalist" prejudice against secular science. I take a literalist position on creation because, upon investigation of the exegetical argument, I found that this view was consistent with the rest of SCRIPTURE, without apologies to science. And the literalist position is also consistent with the Westminster Confession of Faith which states clearly and concisely, "... the space of six days ..." (Chap. IV, para. 1).

LITERALISM AND THE LAW

However, I wasn't always a literalist on Genesis 1. The textual stumbling block to my previous belief in the "day-age" theory came from within the 10 Commandments, "For in six days the LORD made heaven and earth, the sea, and all that in them is, and rested the seventh day: wherefore the LORD blessed the Sabbath day, and hallowed it" (*Ex. 20:11*). It could not be ignored in understanding. When that hurdle was cleared by the blast from Moses' interpretation, I accepted the literal understanding of the creation account. Only then does the Genesis account square with the Exodus text and give me understanding of what the Sabbath means for my life, my family, and the life of my congregation.

The issue of the literalness of the creation account is no slight matter, especially for the life and work of the church. Without the literal, six-day creation, there is no theology to justify the keeping of either the Old Covenant Sabbath or the New Covenant Sabbath, *i.e.*, the Lord's Day. That's the very point of Moses' literal explanation reminding us to keep the Sabbath day.

Before dealing with this literal application for the local church, a brief argument for the perpetuity of the Sabbath command is important. *First*, the text of Deuteronomy 4[1] calls this moral law "his covenant," implying a singular covenant written in 10 "words"[2] — again reinforcing solidarity of the fourth word/commandment along with the other "words" of the covenant. The fourth word cannot be extrapolated without doing damage to this covenant structure itself. Some have suggested that the fourth word is a ceremonial law in the midst of the moral law. Michael Horton argues that this commandment "belongs" in the ceremonial part of the law "rather than the moral part." But where one would rather relocate this law is irrelevant to the fact that it is NOT in the midst of ceremonies but in the heart of the moral law — within the depths of the 10 words of this singular covenant.

Second, the Sabbath is commanded and hallowed by God as part and parcel of the six previous days of the creation account; it can no more be removed than any other day of the week can be dropped from the creation. It is a "creation ordinance" made for man (*i.e.*, mankind — not Jewish man or Christian man).[4] There is nothing inherently ceremonial in God's blessing this day; its peculiar ordination as His day of rest transcends the peculiarities of both old and new covenants.

Third, in the light of Mark 2:28 Jesus asserts His messianic lordship over the Sabbath day. His reference to the "Son of Man's"[5] lordship extends His messianic rule over this creation ordinance for purposes of redemptive rulership, not extinction of that day. There's nothing implied in Christ's lordship to expunge the fourth word from the midst of the moral law.

With the assertion of His messianic lordship, He introduces us to the New Covenant theocratic kingdom which was about to be inaugurated by His "first day of the week" resurrection. As Messianic Lord, He is not bound to the old ceremonies, nor to the specific "end-of-the-week" mode; but instead makes that commandment serve His new theocratic purposes: resurrection on the First Day of the week — and all for the new theocratic kingdom and church called a new creation.

It is the day of the church, the day in which we do the highest and most sacred recreation: listen to God's Word preached. It is the day when the church can insist that all God's people unite for worship and even threaten wrath to those in the covenant community who forsake the assembling of themselves. It is the day most intense in self-sacrifice for the sake of covenant worship. We gather not first for our good, but for God's glory, and then for the welfare of our neighbor. We do not have the right to allow for another day of rest — to accommodate busy work and vacation schedules.

It takes self-discipline to keep the literal regular ratio of six days to one day. It is a spiritual discipline at heart with practical implications of time management. How can the work of the family, the job, the school, the vacation, etc., be accomplished within the interval of six literal days split up by the Sabbath resting? Does my boss have a right to ask of me seven literal days for his work while the work of worship and fellowship gets shortchanged?

CHURCH DISCIPLINE

The proper application of church discipline rests on the literalness of understanding the creation account. If the Lord's Day or the Christian Sabbath (as the Westminster Confession of Faith calls it) is left up to the exigencies of the moment or to individual interpretation, why meet on Sunday? If that were the case, the church could well meet on any day as the holy day of the Lord; in fact, each individual Christian could designate his own holy day, his own personal day of obligation to worship — no organized day of worship could be insisted on. Hence, the Christian would not "feel" obliged to gather on Sunday, the First Day of the Week — individualism even as to the day of worship would reign. Sadly, this greatly characterizes the state of the church today.

The time of the worship must be regulated if there is to be unity in the church. Who knows when to worship unless it be determined by God? How would anything get done in and for service if each member had his own private conviction about his day of rest? The preacher likes Monday; the Sunday school teachers want Wednesday; the janitor organizes for Sunday; and the ladies missionary society suggests any other day, etc. — how do you regulate the organization of the local covenant community? What becomes of the unity of the Body? What becomes of submitting yourselves one to another?

THEOLOGICAL IMPLICATIONS

What becomes of the "first day" expression if not referring to a literal, 24-hour normal or natural day? Without the literal six-day creation, the first day merely becomes a pragmatic convention; it could have been the second day of the week or the thirteenth day of the month. The "first day" could refer to anything; so what if the resurrection was on the first day? If not a natural 24-hour day, it would lose all time reference.

Denial of the literal, six-day creation doctrine takes the guts out of the literalness of the First Day of the week, too. Thus the phrase "the first day of the week" becomes merely a convenient expression — merely a colloquialism with no special significance to the "new creation" or "new life" which Christ brought about on the First Day of the week.

The Fourth Commandment clearly explains the world as created in six days, and that it was God's example of work/rest which became our example: a mandatory, perpetual warrant which carries over into eternity itself — the final Rest. Not all the commandments carry such ultimate blessing as the Fourth. The Fifth Commandment, "Honor your father and your mother," is simply commanded, though God does not Himself keep it. That commandment finds its end in this life.

In Thomas Shepherd's book, *Theses Sabbatia*, he calls these "days" of creation — "six natural days to labor ... not artificial, but a natural day, consisting of 24 hours...."[7] Such literal understanding of the days implies that even as six days are six, full, 24-hour days, so the Lord's Day is also a full, 24-hour day, not merely the day-light hours, nor a day limited to the set times of worship service, after which I can do as I please for my own pleasure. We have failed to realize it is the Lord's Day, not the Lord's Moment, or the Lord's Hour!

The literalness of the creation account emphasizes that there is a day set aside for works of piety and mercy and for rest from all the other days of labor. Its time and form are decided by God. What is a day of rest if one will not be a day of rest for everyone else? What becomes of a day of rest for one if others do not participate in it as well? True resting becomes such only when everyone else is also morally called to rest on that same day.

The literalness of the six-day creation account also means consecutive days, not merely pictures or "frames" of six "days" in which one may rearrange the days as he sees fit. Every six days there is a rhythm of rest and work; if not literal, it could be rest to any ratio of work and rest — two days of rest with five days of labor or six consecutive days of rest with 40 some-odd days of work, nonstop! God could have constructed it that way and we'd have to live that way, but He didn't. He gave us the regular, clock-like ratio of so much work to just so much rest.

The regular distributed days of work and rest create an equalized society. Everyone is commanded to rest equally so. When Israel was told to gather twice as much manna on the sixth day because there would be none on the seventh day, they'd better know that each day could be equally counted on and that it wasn't figurative or "framed" days. There would be no food on "that" literal next day. Each covenant household gathered for six regular natural days and on that Sabbath day there was no gathering warranted. With the severe penalty for gathering on that day, the pious Israelite had better know how long a day was figurative! Day-age? Or 24-hour natural day? *Or he'd be dead!*

In the Old Covenant, God appointed for His people all kinds of Sabbath days, weeks, months, and years. If you didn't know from God what a literal Sabbath individual day was like, you couldn't know weeks, months, or yearly Sabbaths either! The weekly Sabbaths, as well as yearly Sabbaths, were based on the ordinary, regular, literal-day Sabbath. You knew when you would get your inheritance returned but only by way of literal understanding. Your debt would be forgiven in the seventh year, a Sabbath year, which was predicated on the literalness of that original day of rest in Paradise, as explained by Moses in Exodus 10:11.

The apostle Paul required that the churches lay up in store on the first day of the week so that he would not have to waste time and effort gathering funds while preaching from church to church. To know what the first day of the week was demanded a literal distinction of time in order to meet the demands of the apostle:

Upon the first day of the week let every one of you lay by him in store, as God hath prospered him, that there be no gatherings when I come. And when I come, whomsoever ye shall approve by your letters, them will I send to bring your liberality unto Jerusalem. *(1 Cor. 16:2ff.)*

Sabbath does mean rest. The Lord's Day at the local church can be the busiest day of the week; but if carefully arranged need not be so, especially with love-feasts, agape-meals, pot-lucks, etc., congesting the day. Carefully planned luncheons, simple and uncomplicated, can be the order of the Sunday lunch. Preparation must not intrude into prayer or worship time for members. Preparation for meals should be done at home and possibly the night before. Utilizing modern labor-saving devices can save on the excessive labor. Excessive ministry by the faithful few cripples their ability to rest; spread the work: baby sitting, transporting, vacuuming, light-bulb changing, etc. Remember, the most important exercise of the Lord's Day is submitting to His service by the hearing of the Word.

According to Hebrews 4:9, "there remains a Sabbath-rest for the people of God" to which we look forward. Each literal Lord's Day reminds us of that future age of eternal rest. The literal Sabbath coming out of six literal days promises a literal and eternal Rest for us in Christ in the future.

REFERENCES

1 "And he declared unto you his covenant which he commanded you to perform, even ten commandments; and
he wrote them upon two tables of stone" (*Dt. 4:13*).

2 Literally it is not "10 commandments" but 10 "words" of
this singular covenant — one covenant with 10 words,
the number 10 having the significance of completeness or
wholeness.

3 Michael Horton, *The Law of Perfect Freedom*, "... I wish to
make the case for my conviction that the fourth commandment belongs in what we call the 'ceremonial' rather than
the 'moral' part of the law ... [the 4th commandment] is
no longer binding on Christians," 124-5.

4. Mark 2:27-28.

5 Dan. 7:13-14 where "son of man" takes on new prophetic
messianic proportions.

6. Hebrews 10:25.

7 *Theses Sabbatia*, 218.

✣ Chapter 9 ✣
NON-LITERAL DAYS IN GENESIS 1:1-2:4: EXEGETICAL OR HYPOTHETICAL?

By Dave Bush

𝕴n recent years the debate over the length of days in Genesis 1 and 2 has become a hot topic. Since the publication of Darwin's book, *The Origin of Species* (which, incidentally, has nothing to do with the *origin* of species as much as the supposed evolution of *existing* species), theologians have been scrambling to unite the claims of science with sound theological exegesis. One need not be immediately offended at this sort of attempt. Every Christian should be able to read the same story in God's Word (special revelation) and in God's world (general revelation). God is the author of both and He does not speak with a forked tongue. Evolutionary theory has pressured many theological scholars to re-evaluate the generally accepted literal 24-hour understanding of the word "day" in Genesis 1:1-2:4. While the legitimacy of the science with which these theologians wish to collaborate should be questioned, the desire to have special and general revelation comport is a noble enterprise.

Several re-interpretations of the meaning and actual duration of the Genesis days have surfaced since the late 1800s. The most popular of these modern re-interpretations of the creation days are the Gap Theory, the Day-Age Theory, and the Framework Hypothesis. The Gap theory seeks to accommodate the long geological ages of evolutionary theory (see Scofield Reference Bible note Genesis 1:2).[1] Proponents of this theory see a long "ageless" gap that exists between Genesis 1:1 and Genesis 1:2 (thus its name).[2] The "days of

Genesis," according to this view, are literal *and* sequential days, however they are not days of *creation* but
days of *re-creation.* The darkness over the earth in
Genesis 1:2 is due to the divine judgment against
Satan's rebellion (which resides in the ageless gap between vv.1:1 and 1:2), thus the need for re-creation.
One should not miss the similarity between the way
the "theologians" of the Gap Theory read long ages *between verses* and the way evolutionary minded "scientists " read long ages *between stratified rock layers.*

According to the Day-Age Theory, the days are to
be viewed as *sequential* but *non-literal.* Each day is
sequential but perhaps tens of thousands or even millions of years each. To its credit, the Day-Age Theory
offers a correct understanding of sequence in the Genesis narrative. The compromise that this view makes
is that it mistakenly endorses an old age of the earth.
Long ages in the geological record are spurious, and
geared to accommodate evolutionary theory and presuppositions.[3] Space does not allow a full description
of the assumptions that go into radioactive isotope
dating methods, and it reaches beyond the scope of
this chapter but a comment or two is merited here. All
radioactive elements decay at a specific rate measured
as a half-life. A half-life is the measurement of time
that it takes a radioactive isotope to decay by one half
volume into a different more stable compound. This
rate varies depending on the element and its particular isotope. The radioactive element is called the parent material and the element it decays into is called
the daughter material. If a rock sample is found with
one half part uranium (the parent material) and one
half part lead (the daughter material) and the half life
of that particular uranium isotope is (for simplicity purposes) one million years, how old is that rock? If your
answer is one million years, your thinking is consistent with that of most modern scientists. Your mathematics, methodology, and presuppositions don't differ from theirs. What has been overlooked is the fact

that one million years is not the *actual* date of the rock but the *oldest possible* date for that rock. Most scientists make an erroneous assumption. They assume that *ALL* the daughter material present in the sample is there as a result of radioactive decay. That is, it is assumed that 100% of the daughter material came through the radioactive decay process. This is a spurious assumption and cannot be proven by their scientific method. Rather, it is a faith commitment, which just happens to play into the favor of evolutionary theory. Why do most scientists readily accept the *oldest possible* date and then assert it as the *actual* date? This is due to one of three reasons: (1) the oldest date best suits their preconceived evolutionary bias, (2) they are ignorant of the errors involved in such an assumption, or (3) they are deceptively suppressing the true nature of their science. Here is the issue involved; if *God* made that rock *yesterday* composed of half uranium and half lead that *same* rock with the *same* data would be *one day* old. Therefore theological presuppositions play a crucial role in arriving at correct dates. Much more could be said about other factors that impact dating methods such as effects of water on rock samples, open versus closed systems, and so on. The bottom line is that the Day-Age view rightly interprets a sequential order to the Genesis days but then capitulates to scientific methodologies, which are done in rebellion to God's revelation and ethics.

The Framework Hypothesis interprets the "days of Genesis" as non-literal *and* non-sequential. Advocates of the Framework Hypothesis start by looking at Hebrews 4:3ff., as an expression of God's Sabbath rest continuing from creation. The *seventh day* in Genesis 2:2 is presented as non-literal and anticipates that eschatological Sabbath rest that awaits all God's elect. It then argues backwards to the rest of the "Genesis days" as non-literal as well. There is a fallacy in this logic. It argues from the particular (the seventh day) to the universal (day one through six).[4] Further, the theory presupposes a *natural providence* as the *modus operandi* during the period of creation. The sequential order of events as laid out in the Genesis narrative is therefore viewed as a literary device and is not to be taken as literal according to this view. The purpose of this paper is to make a small contribution towards exposing the great multitude of errors articulated in these non-literal views of the creation days of Genesis.

The literal 24-hour view teaches that the "days of Genesis" are *literal, sequential,* and *24 hours* in duration.[5] The debate won't be solved in this chapter, but there are some very important matters discussed here that may help to clarify what Moses intended by the contextual and grammatical construction of his account of creation. Further, the purpose of this article is to convince the reader that a comprehensive and systematic study of various elements present in the creation account *demand* a literal sequential reading of the "Genesis days."

A consideration of the linguistic construction of each of the seven days of creation is very compelling evidence of the literalness intended by Moses in the "Genesis days." The *Theological Wordbook of the Old Testament* notes five uses for the word *yom* (the Hebrew word translated "day"): (1) It can mean a period of light. (2) It can mean a period of twenty-four hours. (3) It can mean a general vague time. (4) It can mean a point of time. (5) It can mean a year.[6] It is the context of a passage that determines which of the possible meanings of a word is to be embraced. This is illustrated by looking at the meaning of the English word "trunk." There are several possible meanings for this word. It can mean "trunk" as in the trunk of a car, an elephant's trunk, a box used to hold clothing, the base of a tree, the torso of a human body, etc. The words that are associated with the word trunk indicate the correct meaning. A child's description of the animals he saw during a visit to the zoo would rule out the majority of the possible meanings of his particular use of "trunk."

This is also the case with the Hebrew word *yom* as it occurs in the account of creation.

Much of the contemporary debate over the literal or non-literal nature of the "days" of the creation account centers around a study of the Biblical use of the Hebrew word *yom* and its Greek equivalent, *haymera.* Such a narrow study of the Biblical data will potentially, if not inevitably, lead to a distorted and erroneous understanding of how Moses uses *yom* in the Genesis account. One must consider *several* other factors to determine the correct meaning of *yom.*

YOM IN CONSTRUCTION WITH CARDINAL AND ORDINAL NUMBERS

The first observation in evaluating the contextual criteria is the association of *yom* with the numbers of each of the days of creation. Of the seven days mentioned in the opening chapters of Genesis, the first day, *yom ecad,* is the construction of the noun *yom* plus the *cardinal* number *ecad,* literally "day one." Moses utilizes the construction *yom* plus an *ordinal* for the remaining days. Therefore, the construction is literally, day one, second day, third day, fourth day, etc. By examining the Biblical usage of the construction, *yom* with the ordinal and cardinal numbers, one can get a better understanding of what Moses was communicating as he documented the creation account in Genesis.

YOM ECAD DAY ONE (GENESIS 1:5)

There are thirty-four occurrences of the construction *yom ecad* in the entire Old Testament. All of these texts make sense when understood as literal 24-hour days. There is *not one* text among all of them that can be verified to be anything but literal. One example of this construction, which demands a literal interpretation, is Numbers 11:19-20. In these verses, Moses uses the same construction *yom* e*cad* as it appears in Genesis 1:5. The occasion is the sending of the quail to the grumbling Israelites. The Lord commands Moses to tell the Israelites, they "shall eat not one day (*yom ecad*), nor two days, nor five days, nor ten days, nor twenty days, but a whole month until it comes out of your nostrils" (NASB). This long sequence of days, one day, two days, five days, ten days, twenty days, and concluding with *a month* declares with vivid clarity the literal understanding of the days in view. This argument is further strengthened by the use of "tomorrow" in verse 18. The quail were to be sent *the day after* the Lord made this proclamation. This was literally fulfilled "the next day" (*v. 32*). Thus, it is demonstrated in this particular example that Moses used the construction *yom ecad* to communicate a literal 24-hour day. An examination of all other occurrences of this construction, *yom ecad,* will give the same conclusion.

The question arises, at this point, does the construction of *yom* with the *ordinal* numbers function the same way as *yom* does with *cardinal* numbers? A brief examination of each individual case as it appears in Genesis 1:1-2:3 will demonstrate the strength of the evidence for a literal understanding of the ordinals in immediate construct with *yom.*

YOM SHENI
SECOND DAY (GENESIS 1:8)

The construction, *yom sheni,* "second day" as found in Genesis 1:8, appears seventeen times in the Old Testament. As was the case with *yom ecad,* all the Biblical texts that contain the construction *yom sheni* communicate a literal 24-hour day without a demonstrable exception. The conquest of Jericho, found in Joshua 6:14, will bring verity to this point. Joshua documents the events of the second day concluding, "Thus the *second day* they marched around the city once and returned to the camp..." (NASB). These events followed the *first day's* events. All that separated the two days was the *night* spent in the camp (*v. 11b*) and the early *morning* (*v.12a*), the second day. Joshua marks the literal meaning of *yom sheni* by highlighting "the night" (v.11) and the "morning" (*v. 12*). One can hear an echo of the creation narrative here in Joshua.

YOM SHELISHI
THIRD DAY (GENESIS 1:13)

The construction *yom shelishi* occurs twenty-five times in the Old Testament. In every case save one (*Hos. 6:2*)[7], a literal 24-hour day is in view. Moses uses the same construction *yom shelishi* six times in the book of Genesis alone. In each case he uses it in a strictly literal sense. In Genesis 34, Hamor tried to arrange for an intercultural marriage between his son, Shechem, and the Israelite Dinah. The sons of Jacob had earlier heard that Shechem had raped Dinah. They agreed to allow the Hivites to intermarry with the Israelites if all the Hivites would submit to the rite of circumcision. This, of course, was a scheme conceived by the sons of Jacob to kill the Hivites in revenge for the honor of Dinah. The Hivites agreed to the circumcision and it was performed on "every male that went out of the city" (*v. 24*). In verse 25 Moses writes, "Now it came about on the *third day* (*yom shelishi*) *when they were still in pain,* that two of Jacob's sons, Simeon and Levi ... killed every male." The healing process for a circumcision is a matter of literal days — not long ages. There is no room for a non-literal interpretation in this text. To read long ages here would make for a forced if not absurd exegesis. Again, the construction *yom shelishi* is best understood as a literal day.

YOM REVIYI
FOURTH DAY (GENESIS 1:19)

Numbers 29 could be treated under any one of the headings from second day to seventh day. It is treated here somewhat arbitrarily but mainly because it deserves mention at some point due to the sequential nature and multiplicity of the days mentioned. In this chapter, Moses documents the offerings for the seventh month. He uses the same construction for the second day, third day, fourth day, fifth day, sixth day, and seventh day as found in the creation narrative. These offerings are dealt with in Ezra 3, 2 Chronicles 7, and Leviticus 23. The contexts of these passages similarly demonstrate that the days must be literal. In Numbers 29:1 the festival was to begin on the first day of the month. In verse 12, another feast, which lasted seven days, was to be observed in the same month and began on the fifteenth day. There was to be rest from the labors on the *tenth day* of the month *(v. 7).* Then each day's sacrifice was specifically laid out from the fifteenth day of the month all the way through to the twenty-third day of the month. All these events took place in the seventh *month.* Therefore, it must be understood that not only is the use of *yom reviyi* "fourth day" in verse 23 literal, but *all* the uses of *all* the ordinal numbers with *yom* in verses 17-35 are literal 24-hour days as well.

YOM CHEMISHI
FIFTH DAY (GENESIS 1:23)

The number of Old Testament passages that have the construction *yom chemishi* "fifth day" are the least in comparison to the other days of creation. It appears only four additional times in the whole Old Testament. One of those occurrences *(Num. 29)* was mentioned above in the treatment under the "fourth day." Another text (*Num. 7*) which contains the construction *yom chemishi* will be dealt with later in this chapter. This leaves two texts from which to choose to illustrate literalness under this section. But the usage of these constructions is so unanimously in favor of a literal 24-hour day that there really is no difficulty in demonstrating the point again under this specific construction. Judges 19 gives abundant refutation to the non-literal interpretation of the ordinal numbers used with *yom* as found in the "Genesis creation days." The story in Judges 19 is of a Levite whose concubine left him and played the harlot. The Levite goes in search of her, finds her, and then they return to her father's house. The father enjoys the company of his son-in-law and detains him *three days (v. 4)*. They lodge there *that night*. On the "*fourth day*" (same construct as in *Gen. 1:19*), which is the *next morning*, the Levite attempts to leave, but is talked into staying the *night (v. 6-7)*. On the "*fifth day*" (*yom chemishi*), he wakes up "early in the *morning*." The father wants him to sustain himself until the "*afternoon*" and so they eat. Then the father pours forth a fourfold plea to indicate to him that the end of the day is near. He states in verse 9, "the *day* has drawn to a close ... spend the *night* ... the *day* is coming to an end ... you can leave *tomorrow*." It is almost embarrassing to give further comment. The italicized words mark clearly that this passage is full of time markers, afternoon, night, morning, etc., to mark out a literal understanding of the days in view. Once again, the non-literal interpretation of the construction *yom* plus an ordinal, as found in Genesis, goes contrary to the Scriptures as they interpret themselves.

YOM HASHISHI
THE SIXTH DAY (GENESIS 1:31)

Exodus 16 marks the gathering of the manna, an episode in which God instructs His people in Sabbath observance. The Israelites gathered twice as much manna on the "sixth day," yom *hashishi* (*v. 22*). This was done in anticipation of the Sabbath the following day (*v. 23*). The Sabbath was observed every seventh day (*v. 26*), but the gathering of the manna took place daily for the six *days* in between. In our own culture, our week comes from this model which God established with the Israelites. This ultimately goes back to the creation account itself (cf. *Ex 20:11*, and *31:17*). It doesn't need further delineation that these *cannot* be anything but literal 24-hour days. A non-literal interpretation at this point makes an absurdity of the text. The Old Testament record repeatedly shows that Moses used the constructions of *yom* in immediate construct with ordinal numbers to communicate literal 24-hour days.

BAYYOM HASHVIYI
THE SEVENTH DAY (GENESIS 2:2)

In light of the Biblical importance of the number seven, it is not surprising to find *yom hashviyi* "the seventh day" occurs more frequently than any of the other constructions of the "days" of creation. There are a total of forty-seven uses of *yom hashviyi* in the Old Testament. The account of the death of David and Bathsheba's child will serve as the token illustration here. In 2 Samuel 12:15, God strikes the child with illness. In verse 16 David begins to fast, refusing to eat any food. Then in verse 18, the child dies, "on the seventh day" *yom hashviyi*. When the servants return to tell David the news, David realizes the child is dead. He immediately washes himself, goes into the house of God, worships God, then returns to eat (*v. 20*). If the "seventh day" in verse 18 is taken as non-literal, the meaning of the text is lost. If long ages are to be seen in this passage, what happens to the real history of this passage? This passage would no longer be a real account of history, it would have to be viewed as a story, perhaps a moral story teaching us something about adultery, but certainly not the factual events of history *as they happened.* David could live without food for only a limited number of *literal* days. Only a literal interpretation of seven sequential, literal days prevents David from dying of starvation and retains the historic truth of these events. A seven-day fast is likely but certainly not a fast of thousands of years. The disastrous effects of wrongly understanding "day" in this text are dramatic. So, too, a wrong understanding of "day" in the creation account will radically impact one's understanding of the reality of the creation acts.

The conclusion of this section is that *all* the Biblical constructions (141 in all) of the word day with the cardinal one or ordinal numbers second, third, fourth, fifth, sixth, and seventh (the numbers that occur in the creation account) argue for a literal 24-hour understanding of *yom*. Add to this the total number of constructions of *yom* with numbers other than those found in the creation account and you will find over four hundred examples in the Bible. In spite of this overwhelming number of examples, Hosea 6:2 still remains the *only text* that offers a possible non-literal interpretation as credible (discussed later in this chapter). Thus *any view* of creation that takes the days as non-literal argues against an overwhelming amount of scriptural evidence to the contrary.

"DAY" APART FROM ORDINALS AND CARDINALS

In the case of the construction of *yom* with cardinal and ordinal numbers, the scriptural evidence is abundant and clear. One must conclude that the normal usage of these constructions indicates literal days are in view. The question arises, what about the cases where *yom* is not used in conjunction with ordinals and cardinals? Does the meaning change? The answer is yes. It is clear that often when *yom* appears without an ordinal or cardinal number it can be either literal or non-literal. In the passage under consideration in this chapter, *yom* without a cardinal or an ordinal number appears five times. Those occur in Genesis 1:5, 1:14, 1:16, 1:18, and 2:4. In verse 5, "day" refers to the "light" as opposed to the "darkness." In verses 14, 16, and 18, the "day" is distinguished from the "night." It is clear from the context that "day" refers to the "daylight" portion of a day. The last occurrence of *yom* in isolation from a number in the creation account is found in Genesis 2:4. The phrase, *bayom*, "in the day," is a construction that lends itself to a potential non-literal interpretation. This construction consists of the preposition *bait* (in) plus the definite article *hey* (the) which is assimilated into the form plus the word *yom*. Both the absence of a cardinal or ordinal number and the context lead us to understand this as a collective number of days treated as a "singular whole" (or a single "period" of time). This accounts for the singular *yom*. In this case the referent "day," of which Genesis 2:4 speaks, is the seven (literal) days of creation as a collective whole. The various Hebrew constructions of *yom* function a great deal like the word "day" does in English. In the English language, when a number is associated with "day," the referent(s) is/are literal day(s). In the absence of a number the day may be literal *or* non-literal depending on contextual evidences. By way of illustration:

Example #1: "Day" without a number = *non-literal.* "Back in my grandfather's day, life was a whole lot simpler." In this case, "day" is a reference to the general time when my grandfather was alive.

Example #2: "Day" used without a number = *literal.* "The day I met the President was the highlight of my life." In this example, a literal day is understood.

Example #3: "Day" used with a number = *literal.* "I'll be home in six days." When used with a number, the sense is clear that a literal day is in view. It is extremely difficult to construct a sentence in ordinary English where a number used with a day is non-literal. This appears to be the case with the Hebrew usage of *yom* with the Hebrew numbers as well.

HOSEA 6:2

This passage is the only passage that uses a number in construction with the word *yom* in which a non-literal interpretation is probably in view. Hosea writes, *He will raise us up on the third day (NASB).* This is probably an idiom for resurrection to new life. But the construction "third day" is used predominantly as a literal idea in both the Old and New Testaments. This text is clearly the *exception to the rule.* To argue against the testimony of an overwhelming number of Scripture passages that *yom* in construction with an ordinal number is anything other than literal demands the merits of strong contextual evidence.

MORNING AND EVENING

Of the seven particular constructions treated above, four of the passages examined (*Num. 1; Jud. 19, Jos. 6,* and *Ex. 16*) have words such as *tomorrow, morning, evening, night,* and *afternoon* in the narrative to help mark out the literalness of the days in view. The associations of these terms function as markers to aid in a literal understanding of the days. These markers are present in the Genesis account of creation as well. The time markers *erev* "evening" and *boker* "morning" give added testimony to a literal understanding of the creation days of Genesis. Often these terms have been used to argue for the existence of the sun in day 1 through 3 because "morning" and "evening" are used in the narrative of those days. The observant student will note that the language of "morning and evening" in day 1 through 3 is a marker of *time.* It is *not* to be equated with a sunrise and a sunset. Don't miss this distinction: a sunrise/sunset is *not* the same thing as morning/evening. God places the sun and the moon to mark out *time,* thus the language, *"let them be for signs, and for seasons, and for days, and years"* (*Gen 1:14*, NASB). Therefore, "evening and morning" exist in the mind of God as a specified *duration of time.* Morning and evening do not demand the presence of the sun. They are *prior* to the existence of a sunrise and a sunset. From day four and on, the fully-ordered sun faithfully marks out a "day" with a sunrise and sunset. Since man was created on day six, ever since his existence man has observed a sunrise and sunset corresponding to each morning and evening, but *it has not always been this way.*

2 PETER 3:8

All too often advocates of non-literal day interpretations appeal to 2 Peter 3:8 which states, *But do not ignore this one fact, beloved, that with the Lord one day is as a thousand years, and a thousand years as one day* (RSV). No doubt, most who read this chapter will be familiar with this text and how it has been used to justify a non-literal understanding of the days in Genesis. Typically only a portion of this verse is quoted. Normally that portion quoted is, *"with the Lord a day is as a thousand years."* This portion is cited to accommodate longer ages in the Genesis account. Note carefully two facts: first, the verse goes on to say that a *thousand years is as one day* as well. Most people reject an instantaneous creation, as Augustine believed. Yet, by appealing to this portion of 2 Peter 3:8, one is *equally justified* in asserting an instantaneous creation, for the verse works both ways. Second, Peter wants his readers to be aware of *one* thing. That *one* thing is that *both* aspects of this verse are true. For God, a day is as a thousand years *and* a thousand years as a day. In other words, the *one* thing to learn is that God is not bound by time but, indeed, is sovereign over it. This is not a verse that instructs us on how to view the duration of the creation days.

The beauty of God's Word is that He does give us clear instruction as to what He considers as the duration of a day in His mind. In John 11:9, Jesus asks the question "are there *not* twelve hours in a day." In this verse Jesus makes it very clear just how long a day really is. Christ could have used three words for "not" in this sentence. His choice is calculated and precise. He could have used the Greek word "*may*," in which case He would be expecting a "no" answer in response to His question. He could have used "*oux*," in which case He would be expecting a "yes" answer in response to His question. But instead He chooses the emphatic form of *oux*, which is *ouxi.* Therefore, Christ is emphatically pointing out that they should know that there are twelve hours of "daylight." If we project these twelve hours back to the "daylight" portion of the creation account and give an equal twelve hours to the night portion, we have days of twenty-four literal hours in duration.

SYNONYMS

If Moses was trying to communicate non-literal days in the Genesis account, why did he use *yom*, which generally gives the impression of a literal day? This is remarkable, especially if he was trying to communicate non-literal periods of time. Several other words were at his disposal which would have more clearly expressed the idea of the non-literal epochs. He might easily have used *dor* ("generation" or "period" cf. *Is. 38:12; 58:12; Joel 2:2*), or *moadim* ("times," cf. *Is. 14:31*), or the plural *yomim* ("days," cf. *Dt. 4:40*), or *lashivah* ("old age," cf. *Job 41:33*), or *tzamani* ("season" or "time," cf. Da*n. 2:21*), or even *ate* ("times" or "season" cf. *Ec. 3:1*). The Septuagint, as well, translates the days of creation with a literal intent, using the common word for "day" *heymera*. Why didn't the translators use *chronos* ("times," cf. *Ac. 1:7*), *cairo* ("season," cf. *Lk. 23:8*), or *aion* ("age," cf. *Eph. 2:7*) if ages are the way the "days" should be understood? It is apparent Moses and the translators of the Septuagint *both* saw these days as literal days.

NUMBERS 7

One of the tactics that has been employed by the non-literalists is to redefine the genre of the Genesis account. It is claimed that the high degree of repetition and parallelism in the Genesis 1:1-2:4 follow the pattern of Hebrew poetry. From this structure, some advocates of non-literal interpretations have considered the creation account as Hebrew poetry. It can be demonstrated from Numbers 7 that such a conclusion is not merited. Numbers 7 is a highly structured, tightly parallel, and extremely repetitive account. The occasion is that of the leaders of the twelve tribes of Israel each giving their sacrifices at the dedication of the tabernacle. Remember that Moses is the author of both the creation account in Genesis and this passage in Numbers. He utilizes the same grammatical and contextual elements found in the Genesis account but with a much *higher* degree of parallelism and *more* repetition. Note the similarities that exist between Genesis 1-2:4 and Numbers 7.

Consecutive days - *yom* in construction with
ordinal or cardinal numbers
Genesis – days 1 through 7
Numbers – days 1 through 12

Waw consecutive construction – normally indicates sequence (beyond the scope of this chapter)
> Genesis – days 2 through 7
> Numbers – days 2 through 12

Superscription/colophon – summary statement (may introduce a restatement of the same account)
> Genesis 2:4 *These are the* generations
Numbers 7:84 *This was the* dedication offering

Parallelism -
Genesis - (allegedly) day 1 and 4, day 2 and 5,
> Numbers - every offering is parallel to each
> of the other eleven days' offerings

In Numbers 7, Moses uses all the grammatical elements found in the account of creation and yet in such a fashion that it gives us far greater reason to consider this passage Hebrew poetry. This passage cannot and should not be understood as a poetic account, but indeed as a *historical* account of *literal, consecutive* days. Here is an account *in Scripture* by the *same* author using the *same* elements in the *same* constructions and in the *same* fashion and yet it communicates *literal, sequential* days.

Logical Inconsistency

One last problem that merits discussion here (although much more could be said) is a consideration of one of the logical fallacies that is committed in certain lines of thought. There is a logical fallacy in the reasoning of those who argue that the Genesis creation account is poetry simply because it has features that also appear in Hebrew poetry. The argument typically follows this kind of presentation.

"There is repetition and highly organized linguistic structure in the creation account and we know that such highly ordered repetition and parallelisms are found in Hebrew poetry."

Both of these observations are true. However, these Framework enthusiasts wrongly conclude that, because this high structure is found in Hebrew poetry (which is often non-literal) and it is found in Genesis 1, therefore, Genesis 1 must be poetic/non-literal language. By diagramming this argument the error becomes evident.

Major Premise: All Hebrew poetry is highly structured and repetitious language.

minor premise: All of the Genesis creation account is highly structured and repetitious language.

Conclusion: Therefore all of the Genesis creation account must be Hebrew poetry.[8]

By changing the terms but holding to the same format of argument the absurdity of this logic is exposed.

MP: All apples are seed bearing items.

mp: All watermelons are seed bearing items.

C: Therefore all watermelons must be apples.

The logical fallacy that is committed here is called the fallacy of an undistributed middle term. Here is how it is unpacked. In the second example, the middle term "seed bearing items" does not apply universally to either "apples" or "watermelons." In other words, nowhere in this syllogism is it established that only apples or watermelons are seed bearing items. Thus an erroneous conclusion follows. In the creation debate, the universal statement, "only in Hebrew poetry is highly structured and repetitious language found," must be established by the non-literal enthusiasts. If the advocates of non-literal days could demonstrate that as a universal statement, they could make a valid argument. The argument would be valid if the statements could be put in the following format:

MP: All highly structured language is Hebrew poetry.

mp: All of the Genesis creation account is highly structured language.

C: Therefore all of the Genesis creation account is Hebrew poetry.[8]

Of course this is not established in the arguments of the non-literal views. Thus, their case cannot flow by "good and necessary consequence" (WCF 1:6), is illogical, and unsubstantiated. Those who view the creation account as poetic *must* establish the verity of the universal statement that highly structured and repetitive language *only* occurs in Hebrew poetry. Unless that fact is established, a poetic understanding of Genesis 1:1-2:4 is at best merely conjecture. In light of this, the case for a non-literal understanding of "day" in Genesis cannot be asserted *logically*.

CONCLUSION

Several factors have been evaluated here that expose some of the weaknesses in the modern attempts to interpret the days of the creation account as non-literal. These factors are either ignored or dismissed without careful consideration. Much more needs to be said in regards to some of the exegetical difficulties in the passage. There are good solid answers to those questions as well. It is tragic that so much of this debate comes from theologians who won't carefully examine the presuppositions of scientific claims and from scientists who won't take seriously the necessity of the Christian world view to account for science itself. The result is non-literal interpretations of the days of creation. Here bad theology is married to poor science, and the university and seminary professors swell with pride that they have done well in giving us new interpretations that account for "science" and "exegesis." In doing so they have buried the talent of *bringing every thought captive to the obedience of Christ.* What will our Lord say when He returns but "you wicked servants"? We must be good theologians and good scientists for God is the sovereign Lord of both (*Pr. 29:2-3*).

REFERENCES

1 The note reads "But three creative acts of God are re-corded in this chapter: (1) the creation of the heavens and the earth (*v. 1*); (2) animal life (*v. 21*); and (3) human life, (*vv. 26, 27*). The first creative act refers to the dateless past, *and gives scope for all the geologic ages* (emphasis mine). It is interesting that the Scofield Reference Bible was first published in 1909 just 50 years after the publication of Darwin's *Origin of Species*.

2 I will refer to the "Genesis days" or the "days of Genesis" in this article as the seven days mentioned in Genesis 1:1-2:4 *which are connected to the numerals 1-7*.

3 I recommend Chapter 11 in Steve Austin's book, *Grand Canyon: Monument to Catastrophe*, for a brief but helpful treatment of what is at issue here.

4 By universal here I am referring to the rest of the creation "days of Genesis" as a whole, not to every use of "day" in the Bible. I will attempt to show that, on its own, each day will stand the test of exegesis to avoid committing this fallacy.

5 In defending the 24-hour position I have been accused of being too precise. I am not here defending that every point of the earth experienced twelve hours of light and twelve hours of darkness. If the earth was tipped on its axis this would make some areas experience varying amounts of light. Moreover, days 1-3 did not have light in its full telic state as we experience today. I am not defending the idea that the days could not have been a few seconds or a few minutes more or less than 24 hours. What I am defending is that these were not 48 hours, weeks, months, years, thousands of years, or millions of years nor were they minutes, seconds, milliseconds, or instantaneous. I am defending the idea that the "days of Genesis" were approximately equal to the 24-hour days we currently experience.

6 Harris, Laird R., *Theological Wordbook of the Old Testament* (Chicago, 1980), 370.

7 I will give expression to this particular text later in this chapter.

8 The language here may seem awkward to those not acquainted with diagramming language into proper syllogistic form. This is not an attempt to be deceptive but is necessary to determine the validity of arguments.

✧Chapter 10✦

CREATION AND SCIENCE

By John King

*A*part from the Biblical doctrine of creation, there can be no science since a unified theory of scientific knowledge becomes impossible in the absence of a created order or a receptive human mind. Consequently, when secular scientists attack the Biblical doctrine of creation, they invariably cut the branch upon which they stand. After all, since knowledge must be grasped by a knowing mind, it is a personal concept and, therefore, presupposes a cosmic personalism. Thus, for a valid correlation to exist between the mind of man and the physical universe, an Infinite Person must stand in back of the scientific process, guaranteeing both the created order and a receptive human mind.

In satisfying these criteria, however, the Biblical account of creation has stood alone, a fact which may be seen by comparison to non-Christian views ranging from ancient mythology to modern science. Moreover, when this history is examined, these distinctions in the approach to origins are seen to have significant practical impact in the area of technological progress. Thus, while science and technology have flourished under Christian culture, particularly after the Protestant Reformation, all non-Christian religious and philosophical systems have produced technological stagnation.[1] Given this fact, modern science may be anticipated to repeat the failures of ancient mythology due to a similar rejection of Biblical creation. Such anticipations, moreover, are enhanced when the substantive connections between mythology and science are seen.

With respect to these substantive connections, Van Til has repeatedly argued that the only alternatives to Christian Theism are fate (blind law, unity, and order considered as a process) and flux (blind chance, particularity, and chaos considered as a process). Given these limited alternatives, it comes as no surprise that all non-Christian systems share a similar "deep structure," and that modern science therefore imbibes the metaphysics of mythology. Indeed, the distinction between modern empiricism and pagan mythology is simply that between an impersonal chaos and chaos personified. In both cases, however, an ultimate impersonalism prevails since all persons, whether human or divine, derive from an ultimate chaos as the impersonal ground of all being. Given this fact, modern science must be viewed as being more consistently depersonalized, yet identical in substance to ancient mythology. Thus, despite humanistic attempts to stress the formal connections between creation and myth, the more substantive relation is clearly that between mythology and science.

Given this substantive linkage, mythology and science form a single philosophical target and may therefore be considered together. Consistent with this approach, the bulk of the subsequent analysis will focus on the distinctions between the Biblical and Babylonian creation accounts, noting the affinity between mythology and science at each point. Here it should be mentioned that several considerations dictate this line of attack. In the first place, an examination of the formal similarities between Biblical creation and Babylonian myth will serve to underscore their substantive differences, bringing them into bold relief. Once these distinctions are made clear, the substantive connections between mythology and science and their mutual opposition to the Biblical account will be more readily seen. Second, since mythology has an established track record of failure, it provides an appropriate benchmark for the projected failure of modern science. Such a projection, however, requires that mythology and science be linked at critical points of failure which have been previously identified through a comparative analysis of creation and myth. Third, in deflecting the apologetic thrusts of Christianity, secular science attempts to claim the academic high ground by framing the debate as one between "objective" science and religious superstition. The present approach is therefore psychologically advantageous in the shattering of this pretense since it places modern science in the defunct world of astrology and magic. Finally, since a common technique of modern science is to dismiss creation as a species of myth, attacking science through mythology turns the tables, thereby forcing modern science to extricate itself from the mythological charge. For these reasons, then, the bulk of subsequent discussion will concern the comparative analysis of Biblical creation and Babylonian mythology as a basis for a polemic against modern science. Prior to making this analysis, however, the Babylonian account must first be presented.

ENUMA ELISH

The Babylonian creation account is entitled *Enuma elish* and was found as a result of archaeological excavations of the Assyrian cities of Ninevah and Ashur. In its entirety, this epic consists of approximately 1000 lines of text written on seven clay tablets.[2] That the Babylonian account was found in Assyrian libraries (sometimes with Assyrian gods substituted for Babylonian ones) immediately suggests a broader significance for its theological conceptions than the narrow confines of Babylon. Indeed, according to a work by Jacobson and cited by R. J. Rushdoony, there was a common theological conception in the Mesopotamian worlds which provided the background for international law.[3] Given this fact, the following account may be taken as generally representative of the Ancient Mesopotamian world. Thus, the setting forth of this account will serve as a specimen of the more general distinctions between Biblical and Mesopotamian thought.

As the Hebrew title of Genesis derives from its opening word "*bereshith* (in the beginning)," so the Babylonian account takes its title from its own opening words "*Enuma elish* (when above)." Thus, the first of the story's seven tablets unfolds as follows:

1. When above the heaven had not (yet) been named,
2. (And) below the earth had not (yet) been called by a name.
3. (When) Apsu primeval, their begetter,
4. Mummu, (and) Tiamat, she who gave birth to them all,
5. (Still) mingled their waters together,
6. And no pasture land had been formed (and) not (even) a reed marsh was to be seen;
7. When none of the (other) gods had been brought into being,
8. (When) they had not (yet) been called by (their) name(s, and their) destinies had not (yet) been fixed,
9. (At that time) were the gods created within them.[4]

As may be gathered from this quote and as further explained by Heidel:

Apsu and Tiamat were not simply the ancestors of the gods. They represented at the same time the living, uncreated world matter; Apsu was the primeval sweet-water ocean, and Tiamat the primeval salt-water ocean. They were matter and divine spirit united and coexistent, like body and soul. In them, were contained all the elements of which the universe was made later on, and from them were descended all the gods and goddesses of the vast Babylonian-Assyrian pantheon.

In sharp contrast to this, the Book of Genesis speaks of only one divine principle, existing apart from and independently of all cosmic matter.[5]

As the ancestors of all the gods, Apsu and Tiamat first brought forth Lamhu and Lahamu and then Anshar and Kishar, two brother-sister pairs. The latter pair brought forth a son Anu (the sky god) who, in turn, brought forth Nudimmond, otherwise known as Enki or Ea.

Now, as these gods began to multiply, the younger gods became so boisterous in their revelry that Apsu, Mummu, and Tiamat could not sleep (gods with human needs). After trying to quiet them peaceably, Apsu and Mummu decided to kill them (divine murder in response to divine rebellion) against the wishes of Tiamat, the matriarch. However, through magic incantations, Apsu and Mummu were defeated by Ea who slew Apsu and imprisoned Mummu. On the carcass of Apsu (the sweet-water ocean) Ea built his habitation. (For this reason Ea later became god of the underworld when the earth was created as a canopy over Apsu's remains.) Here Ea and his wife Damkina brought forth Marduk upon whom Ea magically conferred double equality (*i.e.*, double power and ability) with the gods.

Now, because Ea had slain Apsu, Tiamat became restless and was prodded by Kingu, the leader of a group of rebel gods, into destroying those gods united with Ea. As a result of this coaxing, Tiamat prepared for war. In preparation for this war Tiamat made Kingu her new spouse (an act of divine incest) and the head of her army. Additionally, she created several hideous monsters to help her in battle. After creating these monsters, she then set out to destroy the gods.

When the intended victims finally heard of Tiamat's plan (a delayed understanding resulting from and thus revealing their finite knowledge), they were startled. Ea was not able to prevail over Tiamat militarily, nor did Anu have any diplomatic success. Finally, Marduk was enlisted by Anshar and Ea to battle Tiamat. He agreed to do so, however, only on the condition that he be granted immutable supremacy among the gods. This request was granted by an assembly of the gods in council (where they also got liquored up to calm their nerves). Thereafter, Marduk would determine the destinies of the gods.

After receiving this sovereignty, Marduk set out to battle Tiamat. As he approached his opponents, he routed Kingu and the rest of Tiamat's army through fear. Moreover, Tiamat herself became fearful when Marduk rebuked her and challenged her to a duel. She nevertheless accepted the terms and fought against Marduk but was killed by him in battle. The account of this battle is most interesting:

93. Tiamat (and) Marduk, the wisest of the gods, advanced against one another;
94. They pressed on to single combat, they approached for battle.
95. The Lord spread out his net and enmeshed her;
96. The evil wind, following after, he let loose in her face.
97. When Tiamat opened her mouth to devour him,
98. He drove in the evil wind, in order that (she should) not (be able) to close her lips.
99. The raging winds filled her belly;
100. Her belly became distended, and she opened wide her mouth.
101. He shot an arrow, and it tore her interior;
102. It cut through her inward parts, it split (her) heart.
103. When he had subdued her, he destroyed her life;
104. He cast down her carcass and stood upon it.[6]

After defeating Tiamat, Marduk imprisoned the rebel gods in league with her and then returned to Tiamat's carcass. He divided her body in two, creating the sky with one half and the earth with the other:

135. The lord rested, examining her dead body,
136. To divide the abortion (and) to create ingenious things (therewith),
137. He split her open like a mussel (?) into two (parts);
138. Half of her he set in place and formed the sky (therewith) as a roof.
139. He fixed the crossbar (and) posted guards;
140. He commanded them not to let her waters escape.
141. He crossed the heavens and examined the regions.
142. He placed himself opposite the Apsu, the dwelling of Nudimmond.
143. The lord measured the dimensions of Apsu.
144. And a great structure, its counterpart, he established, (namely) Esharra.
145. The great structure Esharra which he made as a canopy.
146. Anu, Enlil, and Ea he (then) caused to inhabit their residences.[7]

In this account the earth (Esharra) is pictured as a canopy spread over the sweet underground ocean, Apsu. (Here, the division of Tiamat corresponds in some sense to the separation of the waters above from the waters below in the Biblical account as well as to the creation of dry land [*Gen. 1:6-10*].) Having thereby established the earth between the sky and the subterranean waters, Marduk effectively completed the mythical "three story universe" (which New Testament critic Rudolf Bultmann later raved about). Once this task was completed, he then assigned Anu, Enlil, and Ea to their respective stations: heaven, earth, and under-world.

Marduk next turned his attention to the defeated rebels, reducing them to servitude. However, since their tasks proved so menial and burdensome, they complained to him, and he therefore decided to create man for these tasks. On Ea's advice, however, he modified his original plan slightly: he decided to execute Kingu, the ringleader of the rebel gods, and create man out of his blood:

29. "Kingu it was who created the strife
30. And caused Tiamat to revolt and prepare for battle."
31. They bound him and held him before Ea;
32. Punishment they inflicted upon him by cutting (the arteries of) his blood.
33. With his blood they created mankind;
34. He imposed the services of the gods (upon them) and set the gods free.[8]

Finally, the story concludes with the gods creating Babylon as a dwelling place for Marduk and proclaiming his sovereignty in assembly. In this festival, Marduk is honored with fifty names. Since the last one and a half tablets of the epic are dedicated to this homage, it is obvious that the object of the story is political. Its purpose is to establish the sovereignty of Marduk among the gods of the world and hence the supremacy of Babylon over the cities of other gods. Thus, Creation by Marduk is a secondary motif and is introduced only to enhance Babylon's sovereignty through its connection to Marduk.[9] In fact, this conception of an assembly of gods each linked to a particular city-state provided the framework for international diplomacy in the Mesopotamian world.[10] As a result of this conception, a link was established between heaven and earth so that the fortunes of city-states below were imputed to the success of their patron gods above. Thus, the religious aspect was simply an appendage to political power. For this reason, the Assyrians could take the Babylonian story intact and pompously substitute the names of Assyrian gods for Babylonian ones. After all, with the objective being political power, the gods were made in the image of man, not the reverse.[11]

COMPARATIVE ANALYSIS

Compared to the childish speculation of the *Enuma elish*, the Biblical account is more noble, dignified, and restrained. As is appropriate to the actual account of God's work, Genesis is demythologized and therefore avoids the flights of fancy inherent in mythology. One way of stating this difference is to note that in the *Enuma elish*, the gods are created in the image of man whereas the reverse holds true in Genesis.[12] Thus, it may be seen that the more matter of fact tone of the Genesis narrative reflects a revelation from God downward rather than a strained attempt by man to project himself into the heavens. This difference in tone, therefore, is a most telling distinction between the two accounts which by itself should militate against any theory of theological dependence. Beyond this difference in tone, however, are profound theological differences relating to distinct conceptions of reality. Significantly, since epistemology is grounded in metaphysics, these differences are most germane to the problem of human knowledge. As will be seen, the Biblical account provides the necessary foundation for human knowledge while the Babylonian view, like modern empiricism, leads to skepticism.

THE CREATED ORDER

To proceed in this direction, the metaphysical distinctions between the Biblical and Babylonian accounts may be succinctly summarized by noting that the former posits a two-layer theory of reality while the other holds to a one-level view (a chaotic monism). Accordingly, whereas the Babylonian account sees creation as an emanation of eternal, living matter, Genesis pictures God as transcendent, existing apart from matter, creating it, and ruling over it. Such a conception is implicit in the opening words of Genesis, "In the beginning God created the heavens and the earth" (*Gen. 1:1*). The implications of this verse will now be developed in some detail.

To begin with, since the Biblical creation account shows God to be the cause of creation, the beginning mentioned in Genesis 1:1 refers to the creation, not God. Thus, a two-layer theory of reality involving God's transcendence over His creation is immediately established by a temporal indicator which distinguishes the temporal creation from the eternal, preexistent God. Moreover, because the cosmos is neither preexistent (in fact, God commands it into existence) nor a divine emanation, it is created *ex nihilo* (out of nothing). Thus, another relationship between God and the creation becomes immediately apparent; the creation is contingent and dependent upon God while He is independent of it. After all, God existed apart from creation, but the latter never existed apart from God.

Furthermore, when God's independence of the created order is coupled with the monotheism of the Biblical account, God is seen to be totally independent of anything beyond Himself. In other words, since God is not conditioned by the creation or by other gods, God is *a se*, totally self determined and the ground of His own existence. Moreover, since all finite reality is externally conditioned, God's *aseity* (self-determination = lack of external conditioning) implies His infinitude, even as creation's contingency implies His infinitude. In fact, God's transcendence, as set forth by His *aseity*, is simply the manifestation of this infinitude as it comes to expression in all of His properties. And since God's infinitude is by its nature comprehensive, God is infinite in knowledge (omniscient), power (omnipotent), goodness, and everything else. Furthermore, because God's properties are infinite, they exhaustively interpenetrate one another. That is to say that God is a simple being; His knowledge, power, and goodness are coterminous with one another and with the divine essence. As a consequence of this coterminity, God is exhaustively conscious of His being and actions while He is in control of His being and knowledge. The implication is that this coupling of God's power and knowledge gives Him absolute control of Himself first of all, and then of all external reality which He alone creates. Consequently, His activity in creation is exhaustively purposeful and infallibly executed in accordance with the goodness of His nature. Thus, God's affirmation as to the goodness of His creation reflects a good and intelligent design, infallibly executed and consciously evaluated in terms of His own specifications. As a result, the Biblical creation narrative is seen to establish, both directly and by implication, a good and ordered creation. Moreover, since man himself is part of God's design, his mind is preadapted to comprehend the created order within and about him. The Biblical doctrine of creation, then, establishes the necessary and sufficient basis for modern science. In this respect, the Bible stands in marked contrast to both modern empiricism and Mesopotamian religion which, in spite of their seeming contrasts, are alike rooted in chaos. To place this distinction in a clearer light, the metaphysics of the Babylonian account will next be examined.

In contrasting Genesis with the *Enuma elish*, a significant difference is seen from the opening line. Whereas Genesis traces history back to the absolute beginning of creation, the *Enuma elish* begins merely at some vague point in the past as indicated by its opening words, "When above the heaven had not (yet) been named." Thus, there is no temporal indicator, as in the Biblical account, by which to distinguish an eternal god from a time-bound creation. As a result, a one-layer theory of reality obtains in which creation is viewed as an emanation of eternal, divine matter. It is from this ground that the various gods of the epic spring. According to Heidel:

> The Babylonian creation stories are permeated with a crude polytheism. They speak not only of successive generations of gods and goddesses proceeding from Apsu and Tiamat, with all of them in need of physical nourishment, since all consist of matter as well as of spirit, but they speak also of different creators. According to *Enuma elish*, Apsu and Tiamat are the ancestors of all the Babylonian and Assyrian divinities. But these in turn personify various cosmos spaces and different forces in nature. Consequently, Apsu and Tiamat are not simply the parents of divine beings without having anything to do with the work of creation; but, by giving birth to these deities, they have a direct share in the actual creation of the universe. The earliest stages of creation are thus ascribed to sexual congress. Then after war had broken out among the gods, Ea killed Apsu, and with his carcass he formed the subterranean sea, on which the earth rests. Finally, after a considerable portion of the universe had thus been created, Marduk, the chief creator, appeared on the scene. He is credited with the creation of heaven and earth, the luminary bodies, grain and legumes, and together with Ea, he is said to have fashioned man.

> *Enuma elish* and Genesis chapter 1 both refer to a watery chaos, a feature which is found also in the cosmologies of the Egyptians and Phoenicians and in the Vedic literature. *Enuma elish* conceives of this chaos as *living* matter and as being an integral part of the first two prin-

ciples, Apsu and Tiamat, in whom all the elements of the future universe were commingled, separated into the waters above and below, into dry land and ocean.[13]

As can be seen from the above description, the *Enuma elish* sets forth a one-layer theory of reality in which transcendence is lost. As a result, the world is somewhat divinized even as the gods are reduced to the proportions of the world. And while a one-layer theory by itself would not automatically imply divine finitude (indeed, the Biblical God existed by Himself apart from creation), other factors in the account render this finitude certain. As revealed by the physical needs of the gods, their lack of knowledge, and the deaths of Apsu and Tiamat, the gods are finite. Indeed, if Apsu and Tiamat were the infinite, self-determined ground of all existence (as is true of the Biblical God), their deaths would wipe out the entire universe. The fact that such a result does not occur indicates that Apsu and Tiamat are not *a se* but rather externally conditioned finite beings.

Moreover, when the plurality of the gods is coupled with their finitude, they are seen to limit one another in a fashion that often leads to conflict. In the case of the Trinity, of course, such plurality is not a problem. Due to the infinitude of the Persons, there is an exhaustive interpenetration of the Persons with one another and with the Godhead as a whole. Given the fact that the Persons are coterminous with each other and with the divine essence, therefore, they are each infinitely good and thus infinitely able to execute their good wills within a harmonious Trinitarian economy. In the case of finite gods, however, such harmony cannot exist. As each one is finite, and therefore lacking in goodness, knowledge, and power, conflict is inevitable, even with the best of intentions. After all, if one god cannot control all the factors, he is bound to step on another god's toes. (And in the Babylonian system the gods have toes!) Thus, divine conflict is inevitable in this system. Indeed, in the Babylonian view, it is precisely out of this conflict, and not divine harmony, that man and the universe were created!

Given these facts, it follows that no unified theory of knowledge is possible upon the metaphysical assumptions of the *Enuma elish*. First, since the gods are limited in knowledge, power, and extent, they are incapable of formulating, much less transmitting, an ordered design to creation. In fact, they are represented as working and toiling in a human fashion rather than creating by a fiat-word. Second, given their propensity for conflict, it would be assumed that such gods would often work at cross-purposes with one another in any venture. Moreover, with respect to substance, the universe itself is fashioned from the remains of Apsu and Tiamat, the very ground of the conflict in the story. Thus, the creation envisioned in the *Enuma elish* is suspect with respect to both divine ability and material substance. Next to the Biblical account, then, the *Enuma elish* provides no basis for an ordered creation and, hence, no foundation for human knowledge. And while the *Enuma elish* may strike the secular mind as a joke, it is to be remembered that the *Enuma elish* is little more than a personified version of Darwinian chaos. Thus, in its modern depersonalized sense, mythology is the "bread and butter" of modern science. Consequently, modern science, no less than ancient mythology, is built on a foundation of sand. In both cases, a denial of created order destroys the basis for human thought.

THE RECEPTIVE MIND

In addition to a created order, however, science requires a receptive mind. Given this fact, the human aspect of the problem of knowledge provides a second point at which to contrast creation and myth. Here, the primary aspect of the analysis concerns the problem of sin and its effects on human thought. Sin affects human knowledge because knowledge and ethics are necessarily interrelated. After all, ethics presupposes a knowledge of good and evil, even as knowledge presupposes an ethical commitment to truth. However, since all truth is revelational of God, sinful man will systematically suppress truth and embrace falsehood unless he is regenerated or restrained by God. Thus, true knowledge requires a redemption from sin and its effects. Yet, since the possibility of redemption is related to the nature of sin, the creation and fall of man are implicated in the problem of knowledge.

In this regard, the Biblical account shows man to have been created originally good (*Gen. 1:31*) with sin entering some time after creation. Accordingly, since sin, therefore, derives from the human character and is not intrinsic to the created nature of man or the universe, sin and its consequent effects are said to be ethical, not metaphysical. Consistent with the ethical nature of these effects, the image of God in man is said to have been twisted (an ethical effect), not erased (a metaphysical effect) by the fall. Now, since ethics concerns the goals, means, and motives of human behavior, the retention of God's image in a metaphysical sense, together with its ethical twisting, has definite implications for truth. The implication is that while man retains his created abilities in a formal sense (metaphysical), he is driven toward ungodly ends through sinful means by evil motives (ethical). With respect to knowledge, then, man can still perceive the truth in a formal sense (metaphysical) but chooses to embrace lies (ethical) instead. In other words, just as God's image was twisted but not erased in man, so man twists but does not erase the truth. Given this fact, the chief problem in human thought is seen to arise not from error but from a willful and depraved suppression of known truth (*Rom. 1:18*). Obviously, this desire to suppress God's revelation is detrimental to the scientific enterprise.

However, because sin is not built into the universe and does not characterize God, sin and its effects can be cured through redemption which operates against the backdrop of creation, both restoring and consummating it. In other words, it is the original goodness of creation which implies the ethical (not metaphysical) nature of sin and which therefore makes Christ's work possible. Moreover, since Christ's work restores man's ethical status, man, motivated by grace and in conformity to Biblical law, seeks God as his highest good in all phases of human activity, science included. Thus, redemption in Christ implies an ethical restoration that liberates man from his willful suppression of the truth. Consequently, the gospel is good news for human knowledge as well as human beings since it liberates the human mind to fully embrace the God-given order in creation.

In this regard, a major difference may again be seen between the Biblical account and the *Enuma elish* in terms of their respective implications for knowledge. While the former shows man to have been created good and to be the object of God's special redemptive activity (*Gen. 3:15*), the latter views man as created in a permanent state of evil. After all, in the Babylonian account, man is essentially created from an evil substance (Kingu's blood) by evil gods. Evil is therefore a metaphysical problem, built into the fabric of the universe, and thus an unalterable quality. Consequently, evil is a fact of life (the way things are), and no concept of redemption applies. So, while the Bible sees God as delivering man into the light of truth, the *Enuma elish* leaves man stranded, groping about in the thick darkness of his evil nature with no possibility of redemption. Needless to say, in such a system, falsehood will triumph over truth.

In a like fashion, modern empiricism also leaves man with a metaphysical handicap. As the product of chaos in a meaningless universe, no correlation can exist between the mind of man and the world about him. What's more, in such a universe there is not even a reason to lament such a fact. After all, such lamentation would reflect an impossible desire for man to escape the chaotic ground of his existence. Since man is thus trapped in a world of flux, he is beyond redemption, beyond ethics, and, consequently, beyond the truth. In the "dog eat dog" world envisioned by modern science, it is up to man to make his own truth on the spot as it is needed to survive. A situation ethics therefore applies to knowledge as well as human behavior so that truth is simply what works in the moment. In effect, truth becomes instrumental, not ontological, as man slips into the void. Moreover, should a known lie serve better than the truth in any particular moment, man may cynically rationalize this behavior as consistent with the lack of objective truth and as driven by the chaotic ground of his being. Thus, for empiricism and mythology alike, man cannot escape the built in evil of his nature. In each case, man becomes a helpless, constitutionally driven, and environmentally determined liar who is thus incapable of change. Needless to say, under such conditions, knowledge becomes impossible as truth falls to the ground.

THE DOMINION TASK

Finally, it should be mentioned that the views discussed above impact human knowledge through their divergent conceptions of vocation. To see these implications, it must first be recognized that vocation, knowledge, and ethics interrelate. Thus, even as science is itself a vocation, so all vocations involve knowledge or science in the general sense. Moreover, since knowledge and vocation are themselves forms of moral behavior, the long-term potential of man's scientific and vocational endeavors may be determined by evaluating them against the motive, standard, and goal of Christian ethics. After all, in the giving of the dominion mandate (*Gen. 1:28*), these ethical parameters were set for man's scientific and vocational activities at the commencement of his historical task. Thus, in gratitude for God's creation and exaltation of him (the ethical motive) and in accordance with the law of God written upon his heart (the ethical standard), man was to take dominion over the earth to realize God's purpose for him and thereby glorify God (the ethical goal). Clearly, such an exalted view of man and his task is conducive to a sustained search for knowledge since it provides man with a driving motive, a standard, and a goal for his activity. Moreover, since man's vocational activity is blessed by God in terms of its ethical conformity, the Biblical approach assumes an historic framework within which long term scientific progress is inevitable.

In the Babylonian account, by contrast, man is created for menial tasks in a chaotic world. Thus, he is driven by no grateful motive, guided by no fixed law, and pointed in no firm direction. He exists so that the gods can party. The only difference between this view and modern empiricism, of course, is that there are no gods to party anymore. In either case, however, man is unmotivated and without purpose in a lawless universe. Needless to say, in the absence of a driving motive, a reliable standard, and a firm direction, scientific progress cannot be sustained. After all, apart from a doctrine of inevitable progress, all sustained effort is futile.

CONCLUSION

In the preceding analysis, significant differences between the mythological and Biblical worldviews were considered in terms of their respective epistemological implications. In contrast to the Biblical creation account, Babylonian mythology was shown to posit the ultimacy of chaos and, thereby, undercut any basis for scientific progress. Additionally, it was shown that in terms of the division between Biblical creation and mythical chaos, modern science is simply a more consistently depersonalized version of ancient myth. Given these affinities, then, it is evident that, despite secular attempts to lump creation with ancient myth, the more substantive connection is that between ancient mythology and modern science. After all, mythology and science are alike opposed to the Biblical view for the very reason that both are champions of chaos.

Given this fact, one would expect the two views to produce an identical cultural impact with a pervasive pessimism growing out of their common commitment to chance. In fact, such a hypothesis is readily verified when the statements of their respective adherents are taken into account. In this regard, the epistemological skepticism and fatalistic resignation of ancient Mesopotamian culture may be seen in the helpless expressions of Akkadian and Assyrian worshipers:[14]

> Oh! That I only knew that these things are well pleasing to a god!
>
> What is good in one's sight is evil for a god.
>
> What is bad in one's own mind is good for his god.
>
> Who can understand the counsel of the gods in the midst of heaven?
>
> The plan of a god is deep waters, who can comprehend it
>
> Where has befuddled mankind ever learned what a god's conduct is?
>
> ...O Lord, my transgressions are many; great are my sins.
>
> ... O god whom I know or do not know, (my) transgressions are many; great are (my) sins.... The god whom I know or do not know has oppressed me; the goddess whom I know or do not know has placed suffering upon me;
>
> Although I am constantly looking for help, no one takes me by the hand;
>
> When I weep they do not come to my side...

Man is dumb; he knows nothing;

Mankind, everyone that exists — what does he know?

Whether he is committing sin or doing good, he does not know.

In a similar fashion, a now famous quote by Bertrand Russell reflects the skepticism and hopelessness of the modern worldview:

That man is the product of causes which had no prevision of the end they were achieving; that his origin, his growth, his hopes and fears, his loves and his beliefs, are but the outcome of accidental *collocations* of atoms; that no fire, no heroism, no intensity of thought and feeling, can preserve an individual life beyond the grave; that all the noonday brightness of human genius are destined to extinction in the vast death of the solar system, and that the whole temple of man's achievement must inevitably be buried beneath the debris of a universe in ruins...Only within the scaffolding of these truths, only on the firm foundation of unyielding despair, can the soul's habitation henceforth be safely built.[15]

As can be gathered from a comparison of the statements above, the psychological impact of these views is identical with modern empiricism reflecting the pessimism of ancient myth. Thus, just as the Mesopotamian worshiper felt trapped in a senseless universe, so Russell flatly denied any basis for human knowledge and long-term progress. Given this fact, mythology and science are seen to be functionally identical with each view manifesting a similar pessimism due to a common belief in chance. As a result of this functional equivalence, therefore, the substantive connection between the two views is seen to extend from casual beliefs to cultural effects.

Given these substantive connections in both cause and effect, it may be predicted that mythology and science will suffer similar fates (no pun intended). In particular, it is anticipated that modern science, like ancient mythology before it, will produce technological stagnation and intellectual rot. After all, sustained progress in knowledge is impossible apart from metaphysical underpinnings which affirm the created order, a receptive human mind, and the inevitability of long-term progress. Needless to say, these criteria are satisfied only in the Biblical doctrine of creation. Consequently, scientists who attack Biblical creation must be seen as suicidally attacking their only epistemological base. Yet, in view of the Biblical witness, such suicidal tendencies are not surprising. Indeed, it is the scriptural testimony that all such views reflect an unconscious urge to death. "He that sinneth against Me wrongeth his own soul, and all they that hate Me love death" (*Pr. 8:36*).

REFERENCES

1 James Nickel, *Mathematics: Is God Silent?* (Vallecito, CA, 1990), 6, 14, 31-45.
2 Alexander Heidel, *The Babylonian Genesis* (Chicago, 1942), 1.
3 Rousas John Rushdoony, *The One and the Many* (Fairfax, 1978), 52.
4 Heidel, 18.
5 *ibid.,* 88, 89.
6 *ibid.,* 40, 41.
7 *ibid.,* 42, 43.
8 *ibid.,* 47.
9 *ibid.,* 10, 11.
10 Rushdoony, 52.
11 Hiedel, 125.
12 *ibid.,* 125.
13 *ibid.,* 96, 97.
14 Rushdoony, 47, 50, 51.
15 John M. Frame, *Apologetics to the Glory of God* (Phillipsburg, NJ, 1994), 36.

⇒Chapter 11⇐

CHARLES DARWIN:
THE FIRST SOCIAL DARWINIST

By Thomas D. Schwartz

hen not denied outright, the social and political dimensions of Charles Darwin's theory of evolution have been portrayed by many historians and scientists as categorically separate from his scientific enterprise. Yet it is remarkably easy to prove conclusively that Darwin was indeed the first "Social Darwinist."

Social Darwinism is the belief that human beings in their relations to each other, and societies in their relations to other societies, are all subject to Darwin's theory of the "survival of the fittest" in the same or similar ways as all non-human living things. Despite excellent work by a few courageous scholars demonstrating various social and political aspects within Darwin's writings, the vast majority of contemporary reflection on the subject boldly asserts that Darwin simply was not a Social Darwinist.

A recent example is University of Texas philosophy professor Robert T. Pennock, who writes:

> Darwin's concept of natural selection is often spoken of as the "survival of the fittest" but it was actually not Darwin but Herbert Spencer, one of the first to recognize the power of Darwin's idea and to take on the task of educating others about it, who coined this famous phrase…. Darwin himself was not initially happy with Spencer's catchphrase, though he eventually incorporated it into later editions of the *Origin* [*of Species*]. One unintentional consequence of de-

scribing the mechanism of natural selection with this formula was that many assumed that being *fitter* meant that those who survived the struggle were *better* than those who fell by the wayside.... This pervasive misunderstanding arising from the colloquial uses of the terms led many people to take a particularly unsympathetic view of the downtrodden persons in society, which was not at all warranted by the theory.[1]

As this quotation demonstrates, little headway has been made in reforming the widely held view of Darwin as a non-ideological and non-political scientist or in understanding his doctrine of natural selection as essentially Social Darwinist. In cases where Darwin's social and political dimensions are too obvious to be ignored, cornered court historians often dismiss this appearance as merely an example of a commonly held ideology and, therefore, of little import.

For the most part, the relation of Darwin to Social Darwinism has been studiously ignored. Barry Barnes and Steven Shapin rightfully note that the literature on this topic is "impoverished."[2] When the relationship is considered, even superficially, the general impression given by the secondary literature — as evidenced by the Pennock example — is that Darwin's theory of natural selection was one thing, and Social Darwinism was altogether different. As Shapin and Barnes so cleverly put it: "...we can conclude this brief survey by observing that Darwin's defense is far better staffed and funded than its opposition."[3]

Court historians argue that Darwin was a great man and scientist and, therefore, a "pure" thinker. He certainly could not be a Social Darwinist! Much ink has been used to defend Darwin's character in the eyes of his many atheist, humanist, and liberal admirers by claiming that he created his theory for "purely scientific purposes." The philosophical problems inherent in a debate over states of mind, or motives and beliefs[4] do not seem to have bothered those who tackle the problem in this manner. Barnes and Shapin observe:

> The defense in the Darwin case has rested upon three assertions. The first is that of internal purity: Darwin's *intentions* and *beliefs* in 1859 were innocent of "ideological" taint....[5]

More sophisticated commentators ultimately rest their case on the claim that Darwin worked as a true scientist, Barnes and Shapin write, gathering data in a neutral and scientific manner: "The second [defense] is purity of ancestry: 'influences' upon the *Origin* were entirely wholesome and reputable...." Implicit in this asserted innocence is the claim that the theory of natural selection is scientific, and hence value-free, while the Social Darwinism promulgated a perverted social theory by somehow abusing science.

Social theory is taken to be a non-scientific enterprise, which in this case distorts the pure work of the scientist for evil political purposes, according to Barnes and Shapin:

> The third assertion is purity of germ-plasm: nothing untoward could *properly* be deduced from the theory of the *Origin*; truth does not blend with error; insofar as truth was used to justify social Darwinism, it was misused.[6]

Despite the unfortunate effectiveness of these pathetically weak denials, the historical evidence is unimpeachable. Darwin clearly promulgated a race-driven version of evolutionary theory as applied to humans. He believed that the nations and races of humanity were locked in a struggle for survival and that only the fittest — the *white* races — would survive. And, by logical extension, only the strongest white race would ultimately dominate world politics.

Demonstration of this needlessly controversial view of Darwin's social theory is simple. Consider the following portion of Darwin's letter to William Graham in 1881, which chillingly anticipates the efforts of his later disciples, including Adolf Hitler:

> I could show fight on natural selection having done and doing more for the progress of civilization than you seem inclined to admit. Remember what risk the nations of Europe ran, not so many centuries ago, of being overwhelmed by the Turks, and how ridiculous such an idea now is! *Looking to the world at no very distant date, what an endless number of lower races will have to be eliminated by higher civilized races throughout the world.*[7]

Darwin understood the colonial ambitions of the European nations in terms of an unavoidable and unalterable evolutionary struggle. In fact, he saw the overpowering of the indigenous peoples, whom he called "savages," as overwhelming proof that they were racially inferior:

> At the present day civilized nations are everywhere supplanting barbarous nations, excepting where the climate opposes a deadly barrier; and they succeed mainly, though not exclusively, through their arts, which are not products of the intellect. It is, therefore, highly probable that with mankind the intellectual faculties have been mainly and gradually perfected through natural selection.[8]

In the paragraph immediately following this one, Darwin describes native populations as ranked close, in evolutionary development, to apes: "Apes are much given to imitation, as are the lowest savages...."[9] This juxtaposition is not accidental, for in viewing the colonial wars as the mechanical progression of natural selection, Darwin's theory logically placed the indigenous peoples on the level, or as close as possible to the level, of the animal.

The idea that the annihilation of native populations could be understood in terms of a battle of national or individual racial strengths was not a new one for Darwin and may have even preceded the development of his evolutionary theory. In an early work, he writes:

> Wherever the European has trod, death seems to pursue the aboriginal.... The varieties of man seem to act on each other in the same way as different species of animals — the stronger always extirpating the weaker.[10]

Lest one misunderstand the phrase "supplanting barbarous nations," and assume that this indicates the abstract viewpoint of one unacquainted with the historical exigencies of the colonization process, one need only attend Darwin's misgivings over what he himself describes as the "extermination" of indigenous peoples to know otherwise:

> This [the extermination of the male Indians] is a dark picture; but how much more shocking is the unquestionable fact, that all the women who appear above twenty years old are massacred in cold blood! When I exclaimed that this appeared rather inhuman, he answered, "Why, what can be done? They breed so!"

> Every one here is fully convinced that this is the most just war, because it is against barbarians. Who would believe in this age that such atrocities could be committed in a Christian civilized country?[11]

Despite these sentiments voiced, Darwin acknowledged that the "just war" ideology was rational to some extent, or at least understandable:

This expression ["the most just war, because it is against barbarians"] it must be confessed, is very natural, for till lately, neither man, woman, nor horse, was safe....[12]

Later on, Darwin reflects that the domination of native populations is cruel, but ultimately necessary:

All the aborigines have been removed to an island.... This most cruel step seems to have been quite unavoidable, as the only means of stopping ... robberies ... murders....[13]

Darwin saw indigenous peoples as lower, or perhaps degenerated, forms of humanity. However, he does place them one step above criminals! Unlike criminals, the depravity of native populations at least is not willful:

...the brightest tints on the surrounding woods could not make me forget that forty hardened ... [criminals] were ceasing from their labours, like the slaves from Africa, yet without their holy claim for compassion.[14]

Thus the claim that Darwin was no Social Darwinist is clearly just plain false. Yet in his 1985 article, "Darwinism *Is* Social," Robert M. Young waxes despondent over the current state of Darwinian scholarship:

...I want to begin by registering a certain weariness, even impatience, that it's still necessary to argue that: first, the intellectual origins of the theory of evolution by natural selection are inseparable from social, economic and ideological issues in nineteenth-century Britain ... second, the substance of the theory was, and remains, part of the wider philosophy of nature, God, and society, where conceptions of nature and God are themselves changing in complex ways which are integral to the changing social order; and third, the extrapolations from Darwinism to either humanity or society are not separable from Darwin's own views, nor are they chronologically subsequent. They are integral.[15]

Young may be excused for his tiredness, for he himself wrote on the topic a "dozen times" between 1968 and 1973. He indicates that he felt like a "Rip Van Winkle" who in the 1980s woke to find the field unchanged in its prejudice that Darwin should not be associated with Social Darwinism.[16]

In attempting to clarify the problem for himself, Young writes that he thinks that the idealized picture of science and an obsolete view of history has hampered an accurate appraisal of Darwin:

> The zeal with which current scientists-historians seek to separate Darwin's genius and achievements from the work, ideas, and influences of Spencer, Chambers, and Wallace seems to me to betray a pathetic, sycophantic hagiography — Great Man history — which I had thought was waning in the history of science....[17]

Given Darwin's overwhelming importance in the history and philosophy of modern science, it is not difficult to comprehend why his image has so far resisted the wrinkles of his particular story. Darwin is portrayed as one of the giants of science and, for many of his admirers, has symbolized what is best in science. Since Darwin's work is currently revered as an example of superior science, the denials of "impurity" or the only slightly more honest dismissal of the social and political aspects of his theory as quaint artifacts of a less enlightened age reveal a view of Darwin that is, at the very least, historically untenable and, at the worst, deliberately deceptive.

The herculean efforts of Darwin's disciples to deny outright or divorce his crass ethnic prejudices and racism from his theory of evolution are understandable, particularly given their belief that atheism, humanism, and liberalism produce benign political administrations and enlightened societies. It is an understatement indeed to write that the historical reality is far different. Darwin was the first Social Darwinist, and his doctrine of the "survival of the fittest" provided a scientific basis and philosophical foundation for the destruction of multiple millions of persons in the totalitarian regimes of the twentieth century. If Darwin is to be given credit for his dubious scientific achievements, it is only fair to consider them in light of the disastrous consequences of his theory.

REFERENCES

1 Robert T. Pennock, *Tower of Babel: The Evidence against the New Creationism* (Cambridge, MA, 1999), 97 (emphasis in the original).

2 Natural *Order: Historical Studies of Scientific Culture,* Barry Barnes and Steven Shapin, eds. (Beverly Hills, CA, 1979), 125. See also 127.

3 *ibid.,* 133.

4 *ibid.,* 135.

5 *ibid.,* 127.

6 *ibid.*

7 Charles Darwin to William Graham, Down, July 3, 1881. *The Life and Letters of Charles Darwin,* Francis Darwin, ed., 3 Vol. (London: John Murray, 1888), 1:316, quoted in John C. Greene, *Science, Ideology and World View* (Berkeley, California, 1981), 122 (emphasis added).

8 Charles Darwin, *The Descent of Man, and Selection in Relation to Sex*, introduction by John Tyler Bonner and Robert M. May, 2 Vols. (Princeton, NJ, 1981), 1:160.

9 *ibid.,* 1:161.

10 Charles Darwin, *Journal of Researches into the Geology and Natural History of the Various Countries Visited During the Voyage of the H.M.S. Beagle Round the World* (London, 1906), 418-419.

11 *ibid.,* 97.

12 *ibid.,* 114.

13 *ibid.,* 430.

14 *ibid.,* 424.

15 The *Darwinian Heritage*, David Kohn, ed., (Princeton, NJ, 1985), 609.

16 *ibid.,* 633.

17 *ibid.*

✦Chapter 12✦

THE RECONSTRUCTIONIST VIEW OF SCIENCE

by C. Paul Ferroni

*A*ny attempt to discuss a consistent Christian view of science must begin with a recognition of the radical difference between fallen man's approach to scientific inquiry and redeemed man's approach. Perhaps one of the clearest and most consistent messages coming from the Reconstruction movement, in particular, and the Reformation, in general, is that of the implications and nature of the fall of man; specifically, the nature of sin described in Genesis 3:5: "For God doth know that in the day ye eat thereof, then your eyes shall be opened, and ye shall be as gods, knowing good and evil," *i.e.,* self-determination of the standards of good and evil (humanism) versus submission to the sovereignty of God and His law-word. Man's attempt to be God does not stop in the ethical realm (determining for himself good and evil), but clearly is made manifest in all areas of life, including the pursuit of science.

Whereas the Christian sees God being more clearly revealed in every bit of data, the world actively seeks to eliminate God from all areas of thought and suppresses the innate knowledge of God by a secular, self-conscious interpretation of data. Everything is defined in terms of self, brute existence, and chance. This presuppositional base obviously greatly affects the ability to learn any true knowledge in the pursuit of science.

With this basic dichotomy of worldviews in mind, what is science? One possible definition is the pursuit of knowledge from creation resulting from the application of reason to "raw" data, so as to analyze trends, uncover principles of operation, and predict future results. There are at least two basic presuppositions (axioms) implied in this pursuit: (1) the assumption that something exists that can be studied, and (2) that reason (*i.e.*, what goes on inside our heads: logic, mathematics, etc.) correlates somehow with creation (*i.e.*, what goes on outside our heads: physics, economics, etc.). In the understanding of both of these axioms, Christians and the world radically differ. We start at fundamentally different points and, thus, end up with different conclusions.

How does the world attempt to explain the first axiom? In virtually every field of inquiry, vast complicated webs of theory and coercion are spun to dupe the unwary so that they are afraid to question the musings of the "experts." So what do the experts claim? Existence began in a "big bang" some billions of years ago, followed by an evolutionary process that has resulted in the universe as we know it.

As Christians, we have a different starting point in understanding our origins. Perhaps it could be called an unfair advantage. The Creator of the universe has told us about that creation. Because of this, it isn't necessary for us to spend vast amounts of energy trying to understand origins. Rather, we can focus on advancing the cause of Christ in all areas through application of newly discovered principles (technologies). The world draws back in horror at this thought, for they view the scientist as the new priest of the modern world. The scientist becomes the source of knowledge, replacing the need for revelation from God, since he can create his own revelation as a priest of his special area of inquiry. Van Til aptly points out that fallen man:

> ...assumes that if the Christian story were true, then the scientific enterprise would be meaningless. Free scientific inquiry, he assumes, requires that there be no pre-interpretation of facts in terms of the Christian story. On the other hand, the Christian holds that the idea of free

scientific inquiry is unintelligible except upon the presupposition of the truth of the Christian story.[1]

Even Christian scientists fall into this trap. Witness Davis Young (Old Testament scholar E. J. Young's son), a Christian and a geologist who believes that several billion years can be found in the first chapter of Genesis:

> The question may be raised at this point as to why ... mature creationism should be disturbing to the Bible-believing scientist. The really sincere Bible-believing scientist should be content simply to describe rather than interpret the products of creation if mature creationism is truly what Scripture teaches. The Bible-believing scientist should not presume to go beyond what Scripture permits for him. If Scripture really does teach unequivocally that the universe was miraculously created in 144 hours a few thousands of years ago, then I, as a Christian geologist, will be willing to stop scientific interpretation of the supposedly one-billion-year-old rocks of northern New Jersey which I have been studying for the past several years. Obviously my only task now is to describe those rocks and to find valuable resources in them. If the mature creationist interpretation of Genesis 1 is correct, I am wasting my time talking about magmas and metamorphism inasmuch as these rocks were created instantaneously in place. [2]

I suppose one could romanticize the notion expressed above, and say that what Young means is that all the fun is gone if we are told the answer, rather than being left in the dark. But I think there is a deeper problem here. Young does not like the thought of giving up the false presupposition that his knowledge is equal with God's. He resists the need to submit to a proper view of science, rather than the "priesthood" of the elite, trying to discover the deep secrets of creation and explain our origins "scientifically" (*i.e.*, objectively, without any reference to revelation). Note how offended he is that his "only" task would be to "describe" and "find" resources. He isn't willing to consider the implications of his meaning of "scientific interpretation" (read: acceptable interpretation to man's way of thinking) of the data.

Starting with God's Word allows us to have a valid starting point for scientific investigation. It is knowledge of a different sort than any knowledge "gleaned" from the creation itself (which is really data filtered by our reason unto an interpretation). God's revelation is *a priori* knowledge. Every bit of it is unquestionable and defines every area it touches. Since God tells us about creation, the information given to us is beyond question. I am not discounting the real need for correct exegesis of the Word so that our understanding is correct, but where God's Word is clear, there is no more room for questioning. Davis Young's father makes this perfectly clear. He says that God's Word, therefore:

> ...must interpret revelation in nature. Fallen man must read general revelation in the light of Scripture, else he will go basically astray. Of course the Bible is not a textbook of Science, but the Bible is necessary properly to understand the purpose of science. Perhaps one may say that it is a textbook of the philosophy of science. And on whatever subject the Bible speaks, whether it be creation, the making of the sun, the fall, the flood, man's redemption, it is authoritative and true.[3]

Beyond the fact of creation, we also know that God upholds all things by the word of His power and that man, having fallen, is cursed. We know that this curse has vast implications in the creation and is the basis of many of the institutions of man. We also know that the redemption purchased by our Lord extends beyond mere salvation of human souls (as infinitely great an accomplishment as that would be alone) to the redemption of the creation itself. Each of these facts has implications to scientific inquiry. All of them are ignored by the world.

What then of the second axiom: the assumption that reason and logic can be applied to the creation? The relationship between reason and reality is a great mystery to the world. Many have proposed naturalistic explanations of this phenomena, but none have been able to withstand criticism. Recently, for instance, some of the best minds in many unrelated disciplines have formed a group called the Santa Fe Institute specifically to attempt to address this issue. Why is it that the pattern of leaves falling from trees is similar to stock market trends? What do macro-economics and chemistry have in common? One of their associates believes that we are on the verge of discovering a new law of nature that will explain the origin of life and how it is possible for nature to self-organize, thus overcoming entropy, the second law of nature. (See Mitchell Waldrop, *Complexity: The Emerging Science on the Edge of Order*, 284ff.)

The humanist must define all areas in terms of himself. As final judge of all facts, he alone can decide what is true, and what isn't. Nothing exists "beyond" nature and, thus, man, nature, and process are ultimate. Van Til calls this kind of man the self-authenticating man. According to Van Til:

> The self-authenticating man has various disguises. He will appear as the "rational man" and demand that the Christian story must make peace with the laws of logic, as these are based on his vision of Truth above God and man. He will appear as the "moral man" and demand that

the Christian story make peace with the laws of morality, as these are based on his vision of Goodness above God and man. He will appear as the "scientific man" and demand that the Christian story must make peace with the facts of science. For these facts must be what the vision of the self-authenticating man says they can be. But in whatever guise he may appear, the self-authenticating man assumes that he is to be the judge. The vision originates with him. In his eyes he is the judge of the supreme court.... If he "finds" anything, it is pure contingency, pure chaos, that he finds. But he does not really "find" anything. He always "makes" as he finds. He moulds his "material" as he goes.[4]

Van Til describes three distinct types of law. These are the laws of logic, the laws of nature, and the moral law of God. Since each realm of law finds its source in the nature of God Himself, we can readily see why they can be used to learn about each other. Mathematics is an exercise of pure logic, yet it can be used to describe the laws of nature. This is only possible because both have their origin in the same personal God.

The implications of this simple truth are far-reaching. First, since all branches of law have their origin in God, they must be fundamentally unchangeable. There may be some change in the administration of each branch, but in their essence they cannot change. Traditional creationists have included in their worldview the need for a change in the laws of nature as a result of the fall in order to account for entropy. Is such a change possible in light of the nature of those laws? We see a change in the administration of the moral laws before and after Christ, and might expect to see a corollary change of physical laws. However the change cannot be fundamental, since all law is grounded in the immutable nature of God. I think it is highly unlikely that there was no entropy before the fall. I would argue that to the extent that the Holy Spirit does not sustain, this is entropy. The ultimate entropy would be if He simply stopped sustaining at all. Existence would cease. God's curse at the fall was the removal (in part) of His sustaining hand. With the redemption, we see the return of the Holy Spirit with a new power, and we also see progress in all areas — both real and promised for the future.

Second, each branch of law may be used to further understand the others. It is easy to see how logic can be used to understand natural law or moral law. Great advancement may come as we begin to understand natural law through aspects of moral law.

Third, since each branch is derived from God, it is also secondary to God. God is not bound to any branch of law. Each branch is rooted in His nature, but God's perception of them is entirely different than ours. His ways are above ours and no amount of reasoning will fully explain them.

As Christians, we understand that these realms of God's law are the fundamental tools given to us to study and have dominion over nature. The reason that different fields of thought are so similar is that they are all founded upon the same law of God, whether in the realms of logic, physics, or ethics. The principle so desperately sought after by the Sante Fe Institute is simply the power of the Holy Spirit in Christ's redemption in reversing the effects of the fall.

We expect progress in science because of the "new" law of redemption in Christ. Virtually all the advances in science that have led to our modern world can be attributed directly or indirectly to the Reformation and the influence of Christian philosophy.

With a foundation for science built upon the two axioms mentioned above, and with an understanding of the nature and source of the law that undergirds all areas of creation, we can begin to develop a truly Christian methodology of science. It is in our methodology that the "rubber meets the road" in our struggle against the anti-Christian methodology of the self-authenticating man.

In summary, since there are, as Rushdoony so aptly reminds us, no brute facts (facts apart or independent from God), we see that there are no insignificant facts – *i.e.*, all knowledge is revelatory and should lead us towards a better understanding of God. Such a view is scorned by the world and derided by secular scientists as some kind of medieval methodology, contrary to the scientific method, and opposed to "objective" pursuit of knowledge. Van Til aptly speaks to this issue:

> ...it is quite commonly held that we cannot accept anything that is not consonant with the result of a sound scientific methodology. With this we can as Christians heartily agree. It is our contention, however, that it is only upon Christian presuppositions that we can have a sound scientific methodology, and when we recall that our main argument for Christianity will be that it is only upon Christian theistic presuppositions that a true notion of facts can be formed, we see at once that it is in the field of methodology that our major battle with modern science will have to be fought. Our contention will be that a true scientific procedure is impossible unless we hold to the presupposition of the triune God of Scripture....The chief major battle between Christianity and modern science is not about a large number of individual facts, but about the principles that control science in its work. The battle today is largely that of the philosophy of science.[5]

REFERENCES

1 Cornelius Van Til, *The Case for Calvinism* (n.p., n.d.), 137.
2 David Young, *Creation and the Flood* (n.p., n.d.), 54.
3 E. J. Young, *Studies in Genesis One* (n.p., n.d.), 54.
4 Van Til, *ibid.*, 135.
5 Van Til, *Christian-Theistic Evidences*, viii-ix, quoted in Gary North, *Is the World Running Down* (n.p., n.d.), 187.

✥Chapter 13✥

"Inherit The Wind": A Lesson in Distorting History

by Jerry Bergman Ph.D.

Critics and supporters both agree that the play *Inherit the Wind* is the "single most influential retelling" of the Scopes Trial (Alters, 1995). The three-act blockbuster play written by Jerome Lawrence and Robert E. Lee first opened on January 10, 1955 and is still running. It was written to respond to the "threat to intellectual freedom" some people believed existed during the so-called McCarthy era (Moore, 1998, 487). The play was later made into a movie starring Spencer Tracy as Darrow and Gene Kelly as Mencken. Later even a made-for TV movie was produced based on the play starring Kirk Douglas and Darren McGavin which appeared on NBC (Moore, 1998, 487).

The Scopes trial involved a challenge by the ACLU to a law recently passed in Tennessee that forbade teachers to teach as fact that humans evolved from lower primates. The play is still enormously popular, and one recent reviewer noted when it was staged in his city:

> The play opened April 4th and was originally scheduled to run only to April 14; however, with the reviews having been favorable and the attendance large, the run has been extended. On the Thursday evening I attended, the 1081-seat house was full, with Scott receiving a standing ovation during his curtain call. I much preferred this stage production to the film representations and heartily recommend the experience to all. (Alters, 1995, 34)

Many persons assume this popular work tells the true story of the famous 1925 anti-evolution trial involving teacher John Scopes (Larson, 1998). In fact, *Inherit the Wind* is a resounding distortion of the actual events and characters of the Scopes trial. The play openly mocks theism, religion, the South, William J. Bryan, and pluralism. Many of the play's claims are misleading or openly wrong. It mocks Bryan and casts him as an ultra-religious right fanatic. In fact, he was not a conservative in the modern use of the term (Iannone, 1997). Bryan was actually a liberal Democrat and supported an increase in the regulative power of the Federal government. In an extensive study of Bryan, historian Robert Lindner reviewed how Bryan's image was changed by the popular media:

> After 1925 the notion that Bryan and Fundamentalism stood for bigotry and ignorance grew until it became the accepted view. Bryan, the shining knight of Progressivism, now wore badly tarnished armor. Over the years novels, essays, and poems, and *Inherit the Wind* helped sustain the myth. (1975, 9)

The actual court transcript falsifies the play's attempt to picture Bryan as a narrow-minded bigot. Distortions made to picture Bryan in a bad light include the claim that he believed the earth was created 6,000 years ago when he, in fact, accepted the scientific estimate of his time (which was quite different from science's modern estimates). Even Bryan's enemies had to admit that:

> He showed a praiseworthy tolerance towards those who disagreed with him.... Bryan was the greatest American orator of his time, or perhaps of any time. As a speaker, Bryan radiated good-humored sincerity. Few who heard him could help liking him.... In personality he was force-

ful, energetic, and opinionated but also genial, kindly, generous, likable and charming.... (de Camp, 1968, 36-37)

Calling Dayton, Tennessee — and by inference the South — "narrow minded," as does the play, reflects an ignorance of both Dayton and the motivations of those involved on both sides. Scopes was not jailed for teaching evolution, as characterized in the play, nor did he even teach evolution; he was a coach who taught math and general science (Scopes, 1967). Further, as a result of the trial, Scopes received free graduate education at the University of Chicago and help in his career until he retired (Larson, 1998).

The *Inherit the Wind* story includes a "famous scientist" (actually the infamous Henry Fairfield Osborn) whom the play implied was not allowed to present "true science" in court. The evidence that Osborn planned to present would today be an enormous embarrassment for evolutionists. It included both discredited ideas and fossils including the fossil tooth Hesperopithecus. Hesperopithecus was alleged by many scientists to be clear proof of evolution, but eventually was found to be the tooth of an extinct pig — see Osborn (1925) and Bergman (1993). This evidence was never presented in court but did become part of the official court record.

Many supporters of the play argue that because it is openly fiction, the facts about the trial are irrelevant. Professor Menton concludes:

Theatrical liberties were exercised in developing the plot, but occasional courtroom exchanges were taken word-for-word from the transcript of the Scopes trial. Unfortunately, the composite that resulted has become widely perceived as a historical account of the trial. But the play is **not** a fair and accurate representation of the great battle of ideas and beliefs that was waged at the Rhea County Court House in Dayton, Tennessee. (1997, 35)

According to the play, though, the Scopes trial was "clearly the genesis of this play" which occurred in a town called Hillsboro (likely a play on the word "hillbilly") which in the play was placed in "the buckle on the Bible belt" (play script, 13). The play also consistently shows the people of Dayton as narrow-minded, ignorant, and rude. An example is the claim that the mayor offered to look for an ordinance that would keep Darrow from even entering the town (play script, 24). When Darrow finally arrived in Dayton, a young girl screamed he was "the Devil" and ran off in fear as if this was the typical reaction of the town's population (play script, 32).

Labeling the play as fiction does not negate the fact that it openly mocks the religious beliefs of millions of Americans. An example is the statement that the town of Hillsboro has "a few ignorant bushes. No tree of knowledge" (29). It includes such songs as "Give Me That Old-Time Religion, It's Good Enough For Me ... It's Good Enough For [Bryan, who then stated] I've come [to Dayton, TN] because what happened in a school room of your town has unloosed a *wicked attack* from the *big cities of the North!*" (emphasis mine, 16-18). In his critique of the play, Menton notes:

> Some argue that criticisms of the type presented in this study are inappropriate for a documentary-drama because historical accuracy is only the inadvertent victim of attempts to "liven up" the plot. It is typical, for example, to introduce a fictional love story in "Hollywood history." The evidence suggests, however, that the inaccuracies encountered in the play *Inherit The Wind* are substantive, intentional and systematic. It is actually quite easy to see a pattern in the inaccuracies, and from this one can make a reasonable guess as to the motive. Christians, and particularly William Jennings Bryan, are consistently lampooned throughout the play, while

skeptics and agnostics are consistently portrayed as intelligent, kindly and even heroic ...
the writers of the screen play *Inherit The Wind*
never intended to write a historically accurate
account of the Scopes trial, nor did they seriously attempt to portray the principal characters and their beliefs in an unbiased and accurate way. (1992, 4)

Instead of condemning intolerance against Christians, the play openly condones it. When selecting a
jury, Mr. Dunlop was summarily dismissed after he
stated he believed "in the Holy Word of God" (play script,
36-37). Another example is Drummond's (Darrow)
words, "All I want is to prevent the clock-stoppers from
dumping a load of medieval nonsense into the United
States Constitution." Stating that people who believe
the Bible should be banned from juries because they
are clock-stoppers who believe in medieval nonsense
is not a conclusion that results from tolerance.

The "medieval nonsense" in this case was the teaching that God created humans in contrast to the view
that humans descended from apes by the process of
natural selection, eliminating the less fit and inferior
races through wars, killing, disease, and similar means.
One of the most bigoted sections in the play is of a
Reverend Jeremiah Brown who is labeled the "spiritual leader of the community" (play script, 19). He is
portrayed as a sadistic, hateful man who condemned
his own daughter for not condemning those he chose
to condemn :

Rev. Brown: Do we cast out this sinner in our
midst?

All: Yes! (Each crash of sound from the crowd
seems to strike Rachel physically, and shake
her.)

Rev. Brown: Do we call down hellfire on the
man who has sinned against the Word?

All: (Roaring) Yes!

Rev. Brown: (Deliberately shattering the rhythm, to get into a frenzied prayer, hands clasped together and lifted heavenward).... Strike down this sinner. Let him feel the terror of Thy sword! For all eternity, let his soul writhe in anguish and damnation.

Rachel: No! (She rushed to the platform) No, Father. Don't pray to destroy Bert! (Scopes)

Rev. Brown: Lord, we call down the same curse on those who ask grace for this sinner — though they be of my blood, and flesh of my flesh! (play script, 58-60)

Rachel was eventually converted to non-theism and, for the couple, the story then became a story book romance:

Rachel tells Bert that she has decided to start thinking for herself, which in the context of the play seems to mean that she will accept Bert's way of thinking instead of her father's. (I can't help wondering whether her new independence of mind will have unexpected consequences, and whether Bert will ever have any second thoughts about having encouraged it.) The two lovers decide to leave town and get married. Love and reason [the play implies] thus overcome prejudice and bigotry. (Johnson, 1997, 28)

This totally fictional account of the intolerance of the ministers in Dayton is, in fact, the opposite of the general situation that occurred in Dayton. In fact, Darrow himself stated:

I don't know as I was ever in a community in my life where my religious ideas differed as widely from the great mass as I have found them since I have been in Tennessee. Yet I came here a perfect stranger and I can say what I have said before that I have not found upon anybody's part — any citizen here in this town or outside the slightest discourtesy. I have been treated better, kindlier and more hospitably than I fancied would have been the case in the north.... (trial transcript, 225-226)

As Johnson concludes: "One would suppose from the play that Christianity has no program other than to teach hatred. At the surface level the play is a smear, although it smears an acceptable target and hence is considered suitable for use in public schools" (1997, 30).

The play claims (7) that Scopes was arrested because of his teaching the material in *Hunter's Civic Biology* which Darrow claimed was "enlightened science." This text specifically teaches, among other things, that there are now "upon the earth five races ... of man, each very different from the other. The first is the Ethiopian or Negro type, originating in Africa ... and finally, the highest type of all, the Caucasians." The text also teaches the infamous Darwinian eugenics theory. After the problem of inferior humans is discussed, the writer concludes that:

...if such people were lower animals, we would probably kill them off to prevent them from spreading. Humanity will not allow this, but we do have the remedy of separating the sexes in asylums or other places and in various ways of preventing intermarriage and the possibilities of perpetuating such a low and degenerate race. Remedies of this sort have been tried successfully in Europe and are now meeting with success in this country. (Hunter, 1914, 263-265)

One of the "remedies" the author referred to was used in Nazi Germany and today is called the holocaust. *This* is the teaching that Darrow defended and Bryan actively condemned. The conclusion that Bryan defended was, in the words of famous anthropologist Ruth Benedict, "the Bible story of Adam and Eve, father and mother of the whole human race, told centuries ago" which she concludes "related the same truth that science has shown today; that all peoples of the earth are a single family and have a common origin" (1943, 171).

Throughout the play, Bryan is made to appear as an intolerant, ill-informed pompous nincompoop, mouthing such gems as he did not want "zoo-ological hogwash slobbered around the schoolrooms" (73). When asked if he had read Darwin's *Origin of the Species* in the play Bryan said he had not "and I never will" (77). This is incorrect — his biographer claimed that he read Darwin's *Origin* in 1905 (Levine, 1965). Bryan seems to be portrayed in an increasingly unfavorable light as time progresses. Larson even noted that one of the latest actors representing Bryan was now "fatter and more disreputable than before" (1998, 264).

No one could read the play and conclude anything but that Bryan was an ignorant fool about science. Menton claims "for a layman, Bryan's knowledge of the scientific evidence both for and against evolution was unusually sophisticated" (1992, 2). Admittedly Darrow did lambaste Hornbeck (H. L. Mencken) for his caustic and cruel remarks about Bryan, stating, "You have no more right to spit on his [Bryan's] religion than you have a right to spit on my religion! Or my lack of it!" (112) This statement is ironic in view of the venom that Darrow threw at Bryan during most of the play. Darrow then concludes that Bryan has "the right to be wrong"! (114). Linder noted that:

> The best example of non-objective reporting was that done by H. L. Mencken, who covered the trial for the *Baltimore Evening Sun*. Mencken, sharp-tongued critic of Americana and iconoclast par excellence, and a number of other reporters acted unofficially on behalf of the de-

fense. Mencken's attitude to Bryan is summed up by his reaction to the news of Bryan's death a few days after the trial: "We killed the son-of-a-bitch!" (1975, 9)

The movie starring Spencer Tracy is even more biased. As Galli (1997, 46) concludes, the movie is a worse distortion of the facts than the play in which liberals are "untarnished heroes and fundamentalists, buffoons."

THE CORE OF THE STRUGGLE

Essentially, Bryan was fighting for the right of the parents to control the schools and Darrow was fighting for state control, a struggle which continues to this day. The Butler Act that Bryan argued for at the trial — which passed by a 71 to 5 vote — was enacted specifically to deal with the problem of anti-religious indoctrination in the public schools. The evolution of the 1920s that Bryan opposed was blatantly racist and sexist. As noted above, the textbook at issue in this case, *Hunter's Civic Biology*, taught that "Negroes" were evolutionarily inferior to whites and openly advocated eugenic policies which were later adopted by Nazi Germany and led to the Holocaust. This is the evolution Bryan opposed.

Conversely, Darrow is pictured in the play as an enlightened humanitarian who has the best interest of the people and the future in mind. In fact, he was also a materialist and a determinist who defended his clients by denying that they possessed free will. Darrow did not want to balance the Bible with evolutionary science; he wanted to eliminate religion from society and replace it with his idea of science and an agnostic philosophy (Johnson, 1997, 29). Those who support the message of the play try to claim that the play:

...is really fighting for an individual's right to think and seek truth, instead of being forced to accept the doctrine advocated by the town and Brady (*i.e.*, creationism). At one point he assures the court, that unlike what Brady contends, he is ... "just trying to stop the bigots and ignoramuses from controlling education in this country." In a very dramatic and entertaining way, this presentation of *Inherit the Wind* clearly delineates the struggle between those who wish to legislate anti-evolutionism and those who strive to keep science free from religious absolutism. (Alters, 1995, 33-34)

As we have seen, this is hardly an accurate summary of the purpose of the play.

THE PURPOSE OF THE PLAY

It is patently obvious that the intention of the play is to mock Christians who take their religion seriously and to openly promulgate a secular, naturalistic, nontheistic worldview. According to Iannone (1997), the play is an "ideologically motivated hoax" to "ridicule Bryan and his followers" and is "bigotry in reverse." The general opposition by the informed Christian community to the play illustrates that those who are aware of it have concluded that it does not "cleanse ... bigotry and narrow-mindedness," as some allege, but is the epitome of such. *Inherit the Wind* is not humorous, nor is it meant to help us laugh at ourselves. It is openly contemptuous of certain groups of people. Laughing at innocent minorities is not funny, it is malicious. The play manifests an intolerance which has no place in a free society that respects human rights. Linder concluded:

The negative impression of Bryan purveyed by the American press in July, 1925, was enhanced decades later by a Broadway play (1950) made into a movie (1960) entitled *Inherit the Wind*. The movie more than the play assailed Bryan and fundamentalism and badly hurt their image.... The movie is a classic case of historical distortion and the manipulation of ideas and characters. Bryan is portrayed as an ignorant fanatic, the fundamentalists are caricatured as vicious and narrow-minded hypocrites, and Darrow is the idealized showcase liberal. And this is the stuff of which stereotypes are made. (1975, 9)

Further, Menton concluded that:

...the play and film are not simply inaccurate, but rather are highly biased.... The historical inaccuracies are systematic and of a kind that presents a consistent bias of slanderous proportions against people who believe the Bible's miracles, and especially the biblical account of creation. (1997, 38)

Calling the play a work of fiction will not excuse its enormous distortions of the facts. On this point Alters (1996, 33) said the "portrayals of the historical characters and locations are so thinly veiled that even those with the most minimal of historical backgrounds concerning the Scopes trial could make the connection." Those who experience the play are given a clear impression of the events involved in the court case, one they often conclude is valid. In the words of Menton, the play "has unfortunately become widely perceived as essentially historical account of the trial" (1992, 4). Menton concludes that this is unfortunate because the effect of the "frequent showing of the various versions of *Inherit The Wind* are likely to have on the attitudes and beliefs of its viewers" is to bias the public against a worldview held by most religious people in America (1992, 4). A doctoral thesis on the effect of the play on viewers found that it:

...has been shown to be an effective teaching technique... in science classes. A student production of the play *Inherit the Wind* ... was presented to the biology students attending two senior high schools in the suburbs of a major east coast city as part of their study of evolution. For ... this research, 50% of these students attended the performance of *Inherit the Wind*, while the remaining 50% of the students attended regular classes instead of the play. [Then]... Thurstone's "Attitude toward Evolution" survey was administered to both experimental and control groups. To assess changes in attitude over time, this survey was again administered to the students six weeks after the presentation of the play ... It was shown through an analysis of variance that the experimental group of students who attended the performance of *Inherit the Wind* had a significantly more positive attitude toward evolution than did the control group of students who did not attend the performance. (McDonald, 1986, 1-2)

For theaters to present this play today is not dissimilar to presenting a play glorifying Hitler's attempt to eliminate "inferior" races to produce a superior race according to Darwin's ideas. Hitler and his henchmen made the sources of their ideas very clear, and their sources included Darwin and his disciples (Bergman, 1992). It is these events that concerned the lifelong pacifist Bryan, fears which history has shown were completely justified. Johnson concludes that the result of the play was to incite intolerance against those who speak up against the "dogmatic teaching of Darwinian evolution." In Johnson's words:

Why is it so hard for reasoned criticism of biased teaching to get a hearing? The answer to that question begins with a Jerome Lawrence and Robert E. Lee play called *Inherit the Wind*.... *Inherit the Wind* is a masterpiece of propaganda, promoting a stereotype of the public debate about creation and evolution that gives all virtue and intelligence to the Darwinists. The play did not create the stereotype, but it presented it in the form of a powerful story that sticks in the minds of journalists, scientists and intellectuals generally. If you speak out about the teaching of evolution at public hearing, audience and reporters will be placing your words in the context of *Inherit the Wind*. Whether you know it or not, you are playing a role in a play. The question is, which role in the story will be yours? (1997, 24-25)

Further, the play has proved "remarkably durable" and "has had a greater impact" on American culture than the actual trial (Larson, 1998, 243-444). This is tragic because the play has done much to distort history:

Many teachers have misconceptions about the history and legal aspects of the evolution/creationism controversy. For example, most people (and virtually all biologists) think they know what happened at the infamous (and enormously influential) Scopes "Monkey Trial," but they usually don't ... [because their] ... views of that trial ... have been influenced far more by inaccurate media reports and the admittedly fictitious *Inherit the Wind* than by what actually happened. Similarly, many teachers believe that the U. S. Supreme Court has ruled that creationism is not science. It has not. (Moore 1998, 487)

It appears that if one of the goals of the play was to distort history, they succeeded marvelously.

I wish to thank Steven Dapra for his comments on an earlier draft of this chaper.

REFERENCES

Brian Alters, "Review of 'Inherit the Wind,'" in *Creation-Evolution*, Issue 37, Winter, 1995, 33-4.

Ruth Benedict, *"Race, Science and Politics,"* 2nd ed. (New York, 1943).

Jerry Bergman, "Eugenics and the Development of Nazi Race Policy," *Perspectives on Science and Christian Faith*, vol. 44, no. 2, June 1992, 109-123.

_____, "The History of *Hesperopithecus, Haroldcookii Hominidae,"* CRSQ, 30(1):27-34, June, 1993. Reprinted in *Investigator,* March, 1995, no. 41, 16-36.

Sprague de Camp, *"The Great Monkey Trial"* (Garden City, NY, 1968).

Mark Galli, "The Rise of Fundamentalism," *Christian History,* 1997, 16(3):46.

Hunter, *"Hunter's Biology,"* (New York, 1914).

Carol Iannone, "The Truth About Inherit the Wind," *First Things*, Feb., 1997, 28-33.

Philip Johnson, *"Defeating Darwin by Opening Minds,"* (Downers Grove, IL, 1997) Chapter 2, "Inherit the Wind."

Edward Larson, *"Summer for the Gods,"* (New York, 1998).

Jerome Lawrence and Robert E. Lee, *"Inherit the Wind,"* (New York [1955], 1969).

Lawrence C. Levine, *"Defender of the Faith: William Jennings Bryan,"* (London, 1965).

Robert Linder, "Fifty Years After Scopes; 38 lessons to learn, A Heritage to Reclaim," *Christianity Today,* July 18, 1975, 7-10.

Leo William McDonald III, "An Experimental Study to Assess the Changes In Attitudes Toward The Evolution-Creation Issue In High School Biology Students Who View A Student Production of 'Inherit The Wind,'" Thesis (Ed.D) (College Park, MD, 1986).

David N. Menton, *"Inherit the Wind: A Historical Analysis,"* (St. Louis, MO, 1992).

_____, "Inherit the Wind: An Historical Analysis," *Creation*, 1997, 19 (1):35-38.

Randy Moore, "Creationism in the United States Part 1: Banning Evolution from the Classroom," *The American Biology Teacher*, 60 (7):486-507.

John T. Scopes and James Presley, *"Center of the Storm; Memoirs of John T. Scopes,"* (New York, 1967).

Henry Fairfield Osborn, *"The Earth Speaks To Bryan"* (New York, 1925).

Contributing Authors

R. J. RUSHDOONY
R. J. Rushdoony is Chairman of the Board of Chalcedon and a leading theologian, church/state expert, and author of numerous works on the application of Biblical Law to society.

P. ANDREW SANDLIN
P. Andrew Sandlin is Executive Vice President of Chalcedon and editor of the *Chalcedon Report* and Chalcedon's other publications. He has written hundreds of scholarly and popular articles and several monographs.

MARK R. RUSHDOONY
Mark R. Rushdoony is President of Chalcedon and Ross House Books.

MARK A. LUDWIG
Mark A. Ludwig is a theoretical physicist, computer systems designer, and systems programmer. He holds a degree from MIT and a Ph. D. from the University of Arizona. In addition to developing numerous products for the computer industry, he has authored several books on the topic of computer viruses and evolution, the millennium bug, and Christian government.

KENNETH L. GENTRY, JR.
Kenneth L. Gentry, Jr. holds several degrees in theology, including a Th.D. from Whitefield Seminary. He is pastor of Grace Presbyterian Church in Huntington Beach, California, and has written several books and numerous essays.

CORNELIUS VAN TIL

Cornelius Van Til was the leding Reformed philosopher of religion of this century, the author of many books, a professor at Westminister Seminary, and a thinker of international influence.

FRANK WALKER, JR.

Frank Walker is a graduate of Reformed Episcopal Seminary, Philadelphia, PA, and of Covenant College. He is presently a pastor of Covenant Reformed Church (RCUS), Sacramento, CA.

CHARLES A. MCILHENNY

Charles A. McIlhenny is a graduate of Reformed Episcopal Seminary and Westminster Theological Serminary in CA (D. Min. '87), and has pastored the First Orthodox Presbyterian Church in San Francisco since 1973. He is currently also pastoring the Hayward Orthodox Presbyterian Chapel in Hayward, CA.

DAVE BUSH

Dave Bush was born and raised in San Jose, California. He has an associates degree in liberal arts from West Valley College; he graduated from Westminster West Seminary with an M. Div. degree in 1999. He is a member of the Orthodox Presbyterian Church and is teaching at Covenant Christian School in Chula Vista, California.

JOHN KING

John B. King, Jr., a free-lance writer from Corvallis, Oregon, holds a Ph.D. in engineering. He is also a graduate of Westminster Theological Seminary West.

THOMAS D. SCHWARTZ

Thomas D. Schwartz is the pastor of Central Christian Church (Disciples of Christ) in Fairview, Oklahoma. He is a graduate of Southwestern Oklahoma State University (B.A., M. Ed.), and Phillips Theological Seminary (M. Div.) and has participated in the Vacation Term for Biblical Study at St. Anne's College, Oxford University. Schwartz is currently completing his Doctor of Ministry degree at American Bible College and Seminary in Bethany, Oklahoma.

PAUL FERRONI

Paul is married to Sheryl, and father of 10 homeschooled children ranging from 1 year to 22 years old, and lives in rural Amish country in Northeast Ohio. He is an IT Consultant specializing in UNIX System administration and Internet security. Hobbies include gardening, beekeeping, music (guitar) and "Civil War" reenacting.

JERRY BERGMAN

Jerry Bergman has 7 college degrees including a Ph.D. in biology and received his MSBS in biology from the Medical College of Ohio in 1999. He is the author of twenty books and monographs and has contributed over 500 articles to professional journals. He is a Fellow in the American Science Affiliation and was an Adjunct Instructor and Research Associate at the Medical College of Ohio. He currently teaches genetics, biology and molecular biology at Northwest State College in Archbold, Ohio.